THE OWNER-BUILDER AND THE CODE

THE OWNER-BUILDER AND
THE CODE
POLITICS OF BUILDING YOUR HOME

Ken Kern   Ted Kogon   Rob Thallon

Owner-Builder Publications   Oakhurst, California

Photographs by: Fred Bauer, pp. 4, 9, 49, 60, 63, 136;
Joanne Bretaer, p. 44; Dumpling, pp. 119, 120, 128, 129, 130;
Bud Emerson, pp. 36, 140; The Everett Herland, p. 33;
Ron Farino, p. 40; Bob Fitch, pp. 106, 108; Jane Galblum, p. 45
Ken Kern, p. 152; Dorothy Real, p. 122; S.H.E., p. 81;
Rob Thallon, all other photos.
Drawings by: Bob Brooks, pp. 7, 153, 167;
Tom Kelly, pp. 31, 54, 87, 97, 115, 154, 158.
Cover by: Rob Thallon
Case Histories by: Rob Thallon
Type: Melior set by Brian, Mary Ann, and Lisa
at Communitype, Eugene, Oregon.

Owner-Builder Publications
P.O. Box 550
Oakhurst
California
93664

Acknowledgments

We are indebted to the many owner-builders and the few building officials who generously gave their time to help us tell this story. Credit is due many people, but it would be impossible to name them all individually. We would, however, like to thank Fred Bauer, Bud Emerson, Anon Forrest, Tom Kelly, Saul Krimsley, John Pateros, Terry West, Bill Wheeler, and United Stand for their special contributions. We are especially grateful to Barbara Kern who, with constant good humor, edited, typed, and proofread each chapter more than once.

Preface

Henry David Thoreau, one of the first Americans to build his own house by choice rather than out of necessity, described the rewards of that endeavor in his classic book, *Walden*. "There is some of the same fitness in a man's building his own house that there is in a bird's building its own nest. Who knows but if men constructed their dwellings with their own hands, and provided food for themselves and families simply and honestly enough, the poetic faculty would be universally developed, as birds sing when they are so engaged?"

Today, 120 years after Thoreau's famous experiment, an unprecedented number of Americans are building their own houses. These industrious people must contend with factors which Thoreau never had to consider. Thousands of owner-builders are presently challenging building officials for the right to build their own homes in the manner they, themselves, determine to be best.

We authors, each of us an owner-builder, feel compelled to initiate a discussion of the issues which arise whenever owner-builders and building officials meet. Owner-builders, from their point of view, do not understand why they should be required to meet the rigid requirements set for professional builders. Nor do they understand why the building department cannot be in the educational business of providing useful information rather than the restrictive business of limiting alternatives. Building officials, on the other hand, do not understand why owner-builders should be excluded from laws initiated to protect the public health and safety.

Our attempts to answer these questions have resulted in this rather curious book. It is political because we feel the issues demand political resolution. It is scientific in order to lend credence to our arguments. And it celebrates the resourcefulness, energy, and care being put into thousands of owner-built homes (both legal and illegal) across the country. We have tried to write a book that will have meaning for politicians, building officials, and owner-builders alike.

We feel that any meaningful discussion between these three factions must result in owner-builder regulations much less stringent than those currently in effect. In the meantime, we hope this book will help owner-builders circumvent or avoid altogether these needlessly restrictive regulations.

Rob, Ken, Ted
Gold Beach, Oregon
8 October 1975

Contents

CASE HISTORIES

Section One
The Code

In the following chapters dealing with the history, extent, and failures of building regulations in this country, we have cited examples from the Uniform Building Code—only one of the four major building codes. We have felt justified in doing so since all four codes are virtually identical in their major requirements.[1]

1. An Overview

Since prehistoric times, people have held the responsibility of constructing and maintaining their own homes. Even today the majority of the dwellings of the world are constructed and maintained by the families who live in them. It is only in the cities and industrial nations that most dwellings are constructed by someone other than the occupant—by so-called professional builders.

Even in cities and industrial nations the percentage of owner-built houses is quite high. In the United States, national figures show that owner-builders account for 40% of all new housing in rural areas and 20% *of all new single-family housing.*[1] Every year in the United States some 160,000 families build their own houses. These statistics underrate the magnitude of owner-builder activity because they exclude thousands of owner-built houses undetected by government agencies, and because these agencies do not report additions, alterations or repairs to existing structures.

It is discouraging, indeed alarming, that there exists no organization of any kind, governmental or otherwise, with the motive of assisting owner-builders to build better houses or of encouraging them to build more houses. The federal government and the building professions, both of which claim to be concerned with promoting low-cost housing, generally ignore this large percentage of the nation's houses which are being built at very low cost. Banks and other lending institutions are reluctant to lend money for owner-built housing, and building codes legally restrict owner-builders to the degree that most of them break the law rather than comply. Instead of receiving assistance, the builders of 20% (or more) of our nation's single-family housing are faced with adversity at every turn.

"Home is a place where one dwells with one's lares and penates, loved ones, and cherished memories; also, it is the face one presents to the world. To advertise a new, unoccupied building as a 'home' is to deny the value of the human soul."
—Eugene Raskin

In this book we are primarily concerned with the restrictions placed on owner-builders by the building codes. It is one thing to be ignored but quite another thing to be legally restricted. Owner-builders can build and have been building entirely adequate housing without the sanction or the assistance of the federal government, the building professions, or the lending institutions. These builders face a real dilemma, however, when confronted with the legal consequences of building their own homes in the way that suits them best.

Owner-builders are confronted with unnecessarily strict code requirements because they are regulated by codes designed to protect consumers from unscrupulous speculative builders. It is important to recognize that the safeguards of the codes were originally intended as an edict to builders whose product was destined for use *by others.* The codes were not originally intended to inhibit people from building shelters designed for their own occupancy. It was assumed that, in providing for their own needs, owner-builders would do everything within their means to insure their own comfort and safety. The breakdown of *caveat emptor* was not the result of people doing for themselves. If the codes were indeed designed to protect the consumer, it is ludicrous for building departments to intractably hold the letter of the law over those builders who are, in fact, the consumer. In this instance, we have the situation of people being "protected" from themselves by government agencies.

A family of four lives in this typical owner-built house. Despite their intention to cooperate with building officials, they encountered so many unreasonable regulations during construction of the house that they are currently building the garage without a permit.

Owner builders differ significantly from professional builders in their methods as well as in their motives. Professional builders have promoted the attitude that housing is a commodity, not an activity. We are conditioned to think of a house as a product that is designed, built, and occupied. Yet owner-built houses in this country (and in most places in the world) traditionally have meager beginnings and contain long histories of additions, improvements, and remodelings. In this vein, building may be considered a repairative activity. Christopher Alexander postulates the principle of repair and piece-meal growth in building by saying:

> The environment cannot become healthy or alive until we begin to conceive the process of using a building as a creative, repairative activity...To begin thinking of the entire construc-tive process as repair requires re-orientation of our current ideas about the economics of construction. The ideas of con-tinual repair and piecemeal growth implies much smal-ler chunks of building at one time.[2]

Unlike their professionally built counterparts, owner-built homes traditionally have meager beginnings and contain long histories of additions, improvements, and remodelings.

Yet owner-builders, like professional builders, are expected to submit to building departments complete sets of plans for their projects before they start construction. There is no allowance in the code for the fact that the process of building one's own house is a piecemeal process, impulsive and passionate and often spread over a number of years.

Psychiatrist Carl Jung, one of the most famous of owner-builders, constructed a home for himself in Switzerland. His project consist-ed of three contral towers, representing the three properties of consciousness—those of outlook, of enclosure and of repose.

Significantly, the building was many years in the making, and, therefore, symbolic of the slow, metered growth of his own consciousness. He says of his project:

> I built the house in sections, always following the concrete needs of the moment. It might also be said that I built it in a kind of dream. Only afterward did I see how all the parts fitted together and that a meaningful form had resulted: a symbol of psychic wholeness.[3]

Who among us may legitimately challenge the individual-right-to-build of one such as Carl Jung? Yet he merely articulated that psychic quality which, he claimed, exists in every person—the house being the spiritual embodiment of one's person and being representative of one's self-knowledge. The ancient Chinese clearly stated their understanding of the importance of the house as an extension of the dweller in the proverb, "Man who finish house, die."

Carl Jung's towers.

The authors feel that, as an inalienable right, everyone should be able to build one's own shelter without unreasonable restriction. We must recognize a homebuilder as a special kind of person—and each person as a special kind of homebuilder. In this regard, no one has expressed our sentiments better than the Viennese painter, Hundertwasser, who states:

> Everyone should be able to build, and so long as this freedom to build does not exist, the planned architecture of today cannot be considered an art at all...What are put into execution are merely wretched compromises standing in isolation and created by people with a bad conscience whose minds are dominated by the foot-rule!
>
> No inhibitions should be placed upon the individual's desire to build! Everyone ought to be able and compelled to build, so that he bears real responsibility for the four walls within which he lives...A stop must finally be put to the situation in which people move into their living quarters like hens and rabbits into their coops.
>
> If one of these ramshackle structures built by its occupants is going to collapse, it generally starts cracking first so that they can run away. Thereafter the tenant will be more critical and creative in his attitude towards the dwellings he occupies and will strengthen the walls with his own hands if they seem to him too fragile.
>
> The material inhabitability of the slums is preferable to the moral uninhabitability of functional, utilitarian architecture. In so-called slums only man's body can perish, but in the architecture ostensibly planned for man his soul perishes. Hence the principle of the slums, i.e. wildly proliferating architecture, must be improved and taken as our point of departure, not functional architecture.
>
> It is time people themselves rebelled against being confined in box-constructions, in the same way as hens and rabbits are confined in cage-constructions that are equally foreign to their nature. A cage-construction or utilitarian construction is a building that remains alien to all three categories of people that have to do with it!
>
> 1. *The architect has no relationship to the building.* Even if he is the greatest architectural genius he cannot foresee what kind of person is going to live in it. The so-called human measurement in architecture is a criminal deception. Particularly when this measurement has emerged as an average value from a public opinion poll.
>
> 2. *The bricklayer has no relationship to the building.* If, for example, he wants to build a wall just a little differently in accordance with his personal ideas, if he has any, he loses his job. And anyhow he really doesn't care, because he isn't going to live in the building.

3. *The occupant has no relationship to the building.* Because he hasn't built it but has merely moved in. His human needs, his human space are certain to be quite different. And this remains a fact even if the architect and bricklayer try to build exactly according to the instructions of the occupant and employer.

Only when architect, bricklayer and occupant are a unity, i.e. one and the same person, can one speak of architecture. [4]

The situation in this country presently favors virtually the opposite of what Hundertwasser has advised. Thousands of prospective owners-builders never get started because of legal obstacles which they perceive as insurmountable. Those who do proceed usually find the codes unreasonably restrictive and sometimes find themselves in court defending their right to build their own house in the manner they see fit. We find this situation to be unhealthy, untenable and in dire need of examination.

Joey and Kate's House

0   5   10   15   20 FT

cost.........$1,500
sq. feet.........420
cost/sq. ft......$3.57

Description

This is a simple one-room frame building with a porch at one end and a wood storage shed at the other. Sections of recycled telephone poles and creosote coated plywood peeler cores are set into the ground to serve as a foundation. (There are three rows of five poles each.) From the foundation up, standard frame construction was used. The exterior is sheathed with plywood and shingled with #4 cedar shingles. The roof is also shingled. The interior is covered with cedar boards.

The windows on the south wall are single fixed panes set between the studs, while the remainder are openable recycled windows. The sleeping loft over the kitchen has a skylight which opens for ventilation. The walls are insulated with fiberglass batts and the exposed rafter ceiling with ½" fiberboard. Wood is passed from the storage shed to the Ashley heater through a small door in the wall.

There is no electricity, so both the range and refrigerator operate on propane. Water is gravity-fed from a hand-made wooden cistern filled by a creek. There is an outhouse.

Comments

The story begins in 1970 at UCLA where Joey earned his degree in sociology. Uninterested in pursuing a professional career, Joey, like most of

his L.A. friends, was obsessed with the idea of moving to the country. He and Kate, a nurse, moved north to a town large enough to contain several hospitals and clinics but small enough to be surrounded by rural land. Kate found a nursing job, and Joey worked in a wood shop where he learned how to use tools. In the spring of 1972, Joey helped a friend build a house and workshop on a large (640 acres) parcel of land a half-hour drive from town.

With this experience and after carefully reading *The Owner-Built Home*, Joey felt confident that he could build a house himself. His

friend invited him to build on the 640 acres, and he began construction the following spring. There was no electricity at the site, so Joey decided to pre-fabricate his house in the electrified workshop he had helped to build the year before. He worked each night pre-fabricating the pieces he would need the following day. By mid-June, after about seven weeks of work, the shell of the house had been completed, and Joey and Kate moved in.

After installing the kitchen, they finished the house in a sequence dictated by the changing seasons. The roof and exterior walls were finished first to protect against the weather. Then the wood shed was built and firewood gathered. The heater was installed, the insulation applied, and finally the interior finish work was started. The last hand-made cabinet was installed in December, seven months after the foundaiton had been begun.

A year and a half later, Joey and Kate started construction of a 560 sq. ft. addition to their house. They want room for guests, for future children, and they want an indoor shower. The addition incorporates two bedrooms, a full bathroom (with clivis multrum-type toilet), a large sun deck, and plenty of storage. It is built on poured, reinforced concrete piers, and it is being wired. (They didn't get a building permit, so the wiring inspection and subsequent hook-up are possible only because the building and electrical inspectors come from different agencies.)

2. History

The earliest known building code is contained in the Code of Hammurabi, the ruler of Babylon in the 18th century B.C. One section of his code is illustrated and translated below.

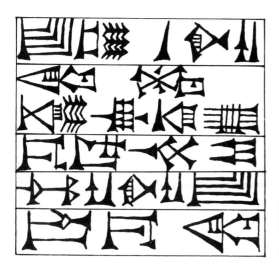

If a builder has built a house for a man and his work is not strong, and if the house he has built falls in and kills the householder, that builder shall be slain.[1]

Early Polynesians insured that a building was properly supported by placing a live slave under each corner post. In ancient Rome, when the scaffolding was removed from a completed arch, the Roman engineer was expected to stand beneath. If the arch failed, he was the first to know. His concern for the quality of his work was intensely personal, and it is not surprising that so many Roman arches have survived.

The Code Napoleon of the 18th century A.D. had a similar prescription for builder responsibility, although the consequences for the builder were not as dire as they were in earlier times:

> If a building, which an architect or other workman has
> undertaken to make by the job, should fall to ruin either in
> whole or in part, on account of the badness of the workman-
> ship, or even because of the badness of the soil, the architect
> and builder shall bear the loss if the building falls to ruin in the
> course of ten years.

In 1189, the Lord Mayor of London required official approval for the construction of party walls; i.e., common walls between separate structures. He placed a high value on the construction of masonry walls which were intended to prevent the spreading of fire between buildings. Although this code was not strictly adhered to, the efficacy of the idea is testified to in the results of the Great Fire of 1666. Despite the fact that 300,000 people were living in 16,000 multi-storied dwellings in the code-built section of the city, only six people lost their lives.

The early history of code enactment in the United States is also related to the occurrence of disastrous fires in populated areas. In the 1630s, when fire from the chimney of one Boston house ignited a number of adjacent buildings, the governor of the colony proclaimed, "We have ordered that no man shall build his chimney of wood, nor cover his house with thatch." For many years in colonial America, fire departments issued permits and inspected fireplace chimney construction.

The Charlestown General Assembly of 1740 adopted a resolution declaring that brick or stone had to be used for the fireproof construction of all exterior walls. Furthermore, all tall wooden buildings had to be demolished within five years of this declaration. Wood construction was confined to use as window frames, doors, and shutters.

With increased European immigration, colonial America passed into a period of rapid metropolitan growth along its eastern seashore. As a prominent point of debarkation, New York City became the most overcrowded of the early American cities. To ease the congestion of the 1840s, shoddy tenement structures were hastily erected. Then, in 1867, in an effort to control the intolerable living conditions resulting from inadequate construction, the first set of U.S. housing laws was passed to regulate living conditions *within* existing structures. Known as the Tenement House Act, this ordinance called for proper fire escapes, a ventilating or transom window to a neighboring room or hall, one water closet (toilet) or privy for every twenty occupants, a water tap on each floor, a roof kept in good repair and a banister on stairways.

One of the most famous violators of the Tenement House Act was the Trinity Church, at that time the largest owner of tenements in New York City. Among other derelictions, Trinity-owned tenements lacked running water on every floor, for which the church was subsequently fined $200 by a district court. On constitutional grounds, the church appealed the fine to the Court of Common Pleas and won its appeal. The court agreed unanimously to uphold the landlord's position, stating:

> ...There is no evidence nor can the court judicially know that the presence and distribution of water on the several floors will conduce to the health of the occupants...There is no necessity for legislative compulsion on a landlord to distribute water through the stories of his building: since if tenants require it, self-interest and the rivalry of competition are sufficient to secure it...Now, if it be competent upon a landlord in order that tenants be furnished with water in their rooms instead of in the yard or basement, at what point must this police power pause?

With no particular thanks to vacillating legislatures or courts, tenement living eventually did become somewhat humanized for thousands of non-English-speaking immigrants who flooded into American cities. Social worker Jacob Riis is personally credited with the enactment of the New Tenement House Act of 1901. This act forced landlords to provide more light and ventilation and more open space around buildings. Building coverage was restricted to not more than 70% of the land area on interior lots and to 90% of the area on corner lots. A minimum of one window was required for every room, including the bathroom. Rooms had to meet specified minimum sizes, and finally, not only running water but a water closet had to be furnished in each apartment. No building, incidentally, could be used as a house of prostitution.

Tenement owners had to abide by these strict housing ordinances for nearly thirty years until 1929, at which time they successfully reduced these requirements through passage of the Multiple Dwelling Law which favored tenement owners. The new law obscured what little progress had been made by early social reformers. The resulting deterioration of people's living conditions compelled the governor of New York, Franklin Roosevelt, to declare that, "One-third of the Nation is ill-fed, ill-housed, and ill-clothed."

At the turn of the century, building construction regulations had been pertinent and applicable only to the larger cities. In 1905, however, the first national building code was written. The Recommended National Building Code was prepared by the National Board of Fire Underwrites, a group representing the insurance industry. This professional group sought to minimize its risks and to cut its financial losses incurred as a result of wide-spread building fires. It proposed a nation-wide building ordinance which would curtail those losses.

Accordingly, fire insurance companies were successful in their efforts to prescribe fire safety standards for all major building construction throughout the country. They were so successful, in fact, that other self-interest groups were soon to detect the advantage of legislative controls on building construction. In 1927, a group calling themselves "building officials" (made up for the

An owner-built fireplace from the late 1920's.

16

most part of building materials suppliers and manufacturers, labor organizers, and other building professionals) came together to prepare and to sponsor legislative enactment of the Uniform Building Code.

There was a subsequent proliferation of building regulations throughout the country. By 1968, the number reached an estimated 5,000 different codes. Most localities either drafted their own building regulations or adopted one of the codes prepared by professional groups. Today, while the federal government increasingly becomes a prime mover for additional building regulation (see chapter 14), influential groups largely from the private sector have prepared national model building codes for enactment by local municipalities and jurisdictions. Beside the National Building Code (adopted primarily by eastern states) and the Uniform Building Code (adopted primarily by the western half of the U.S.), there are the Basic Building Code (claiming to be the most commonly used code in the country) and the Southern Standard Building Code (receiving scattered use among twenty southern states).

Building codes pertaining to single family dwellings were non-existent when this house was first constructed.

The nationally recognized model building codes and their publisher are listed below: [2]

BUILDING CODES

Basic Building Code...BOCA, Building Officials Conference of America

National Building Code......AIA, American Insurance Association

Southern Standard Building Code......SBCC, Southern Building Code Congress

Uniform Building Code...ICBO, International Conference of Building Officials

ELECTRICAL CODES

National Electrical Code   ...NFPA, National Fire Protection Association

ELEVATOR CODES

Safety Code for Elevators, Dumbwaiters and Escalators... ANSI, American National Standards Institute

Safety Code for Manlifts...ANSI, listed above

FIRE PREVENTION CODES

Basic Fire Prevention Code...BOCA, listed above

Fire Prevention Code...AIA, listed above

HOUSING CODES

Basic Housing Code...BOCA, listed above

Housing Code...APHA, American Public Health Association

Southern Standard Housing Code...SBCC, listed above

Uniform Housing Code...ICBO, listed above

PLUMBING CODES

Basic Plumbing Code...BOCA, listed above

National Plumbing Code...ASME, American Society of Mechanical Engineers

Southern Standard Plumbing Code...SBCC, listed above

Uniform Plumbing Code...IAPMO, International Association of Plumbing and Mechanical Officials

MISCELLANEOUS CODES

Boiler and Unfired Pressure Vessel Code...ASME, listed above

Flammable Liquids Code...NFPA, listed above

Safety Code for Mechanical Refrigeration...ASHRAE, American Society of Heating, Refrigeration and Air Conditioning Engineers

Safety to Life Code, formerly Building Exits Code...NFPA, listed above

This building code system, or non-system, has been under constant criticism for more than fifty years.

> In 1921, the Senate Committee on Reconstruction and Production issued a report in which it was pointed out that building code requirements varied widely, and were one source of unnecessarily high construction costs. Since that time, various writers and speakers have repeated these charges and have also referred to lack of flexibility in dealing with new materials and new methods of construction. Much of this criticism is justified.[3]

As of December 1968, this criticism was still justified. At that time, the National Commission on Urban Problems wrote:

> In brief, the facts disclosed by the exhaustive inquiries of this Commission at local, State and National levels...shows unmistakably that alarms sounded over the past years about the building code situation have been justified. If anything, the case has been understated. The situation calls for a drastic overhaul, both technically and intergovernmentally.[4]

We applaud this awareness, but we shrink from the proferred solution (see chapter 14).

Rudolf Miller, founder in 1915 of BOCA, the Building Officials Conference of America, never intended that this situation should develop for owner-builders. Miller stated the purpose of a building code as follows:

> The building laws should provide only for such requirements with respect to building construction and closely related matters as are absolutely necessary for the protection of persons who have no voice in the manner of construction or the arrangement of buildings with which they involuntarily come in contact. Thus, when buildings are comparatively small, are far apart, and their use is limited to the owners and builders of them, so that, in case of failure of any kind that are not a source of danger to others, no necessity for building restriction would exist.[5]

We agree with Miller that owner-builders deserve special consideration under the code. Yet, nowhere in the codes as presently adopted is there any evidence that Miller's principles were ever implemented.

Tim's Tiny Log Cabin

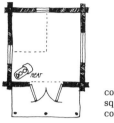

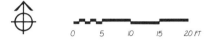

```
cost . . . . . . . . . . . $45
sq. feet . . . . . . . . . 228
cost/sq. ft. . . . . . $0.20
```

PLAN

0   5   10   15   20 FT

Description

This is a one room log cabin with lofts in a back corner and over the front porch. Its plank floor is nailed to four logs supported by various stumps, short pilings, and stacks of wooden blocks. The log walls sit on the plank floor. At the corners of the building the logs are notched to receive each other. The used wooden windows and hand-made pegged doors are framed by 2x6 members lag bolted to the logs. The walls are chinked with burlap held in place with wooden strip nailed to the logs. The roof is made of slender poles bolted at the top and covered with corrugated metal. Heat comes from a small wood heater with a flue that wanders across the room to emerge through the roof and be capped with an old hubcap. There is no running water, and there are no sanitary facilities.

Comments

Tim is a young man with little money and lots of time. He decided it would be an interesting experiment to try to build his house with his own hands. The house, he thought, could be the first in a series of several, each more difficult than the preceeding. In order that he might learn the most fundamental principles first, Tim decided he should use only the most elementary materials and tools in this, his first, experiment.

This comfortable log cabin is the result of his efforts. It is remarkable for its low cost (the only costs being bolts, nails, and other hardware), for its craftsmanship (especially the pegged double doors with carved latch), and for the resourcefulness used in gathering its materials (the floor planks came from the stage of a Grateful Dead concert). At the beginning of his experiment, Tim was bolting everything together, but by the end, everything was being doweled. He plans to replace the corrugated metal roof with hand-split cedar shakes.

3. Extent

Champions of early legislation defended the codes by alleging that safety maintenance, not idle prohibition, was their purpose. "Providing minimum standards of safety" is the purport of the title-and-scope of most codes. This is admirable but dubious. The thousands of pages of code hardly seem "minimum." In California, for example, pages of law pertaining to the construction of dwellings are formidable. First, one must turn to the Health and Safety Code, an eight-volume "revision and consolidation" of laws relative to the "preservation of health and safety." One hundred pages therein is found the State Housing Act, which in turn adopts by reference the Uniform Plumbing Code (210 pages), the National Electrical Code (534 pages), the four-book Uniform Building Code (2800 pages), the Uniform Mechanical Code (275 pages), and the Uniform Housing Code (400 pages.).

A reference to the Uniform Building Code is the 788-page UBC Standards book, and, unhappily for code-hassled owner-builders, there is the 300-page Uniform Code for the Abatement of Dangerous Buildings. The multi-volumed California Administrative Code provides procedural clarification of the other laws.

In fairness, requirements for dwellings constitute only a portion of said codes. But, to fully understand the "legalities" involved in a home-building project, one must consult literally volumes of law. Law books have become voluminous, with statutues controlling both the basic and the obscure habits of man.

We have laws such as zoning ordinances, health (sanitation) codes, and building codes—all regulating contstruction and use of buildings and defining permissable land-use. Bureaucracies exist

Motor homes are presently the only type of permanent dwelling not affected by the concepts of "health and safety" prescribed by the uniform codes. They must, however, conform to highway safety regulations.

to control water quality, air quality, and general environmental quality—all, unfortunately, *post facto* to pollution. With the elements duly "protected," laws prescribe designs and materials allowable in housing construction. Regulations concern all the particulars of a project, including soil analysis, foundations, minimum floor areas and ceiling heights, and numbers and sizes of windows and doors. For one's safety, a section of the California State Housing Law even directs itself to the function of hotplates: "The bed and any drapes, curtains, towels, or other readily combustible materials in the room are located so that they do not come in contact with the hotplate." (Sec. 17921.1 j)

Consider, for a moment, the hassle a New York architect must go through before he can expect approval for a housing project in that city. Plans must first be submitted to and approved by the following offices: the New York City Administrative Code, the New York State and the New York City Zoning Resolution, the FHA Minimum Property Standards, the New York State Division of Housing

Regulations, the Housing Redevelopment Board of Regulations, the Public Housing Administration Regulation, and the Community Facilities Administration Regulation. The architect must then seek acceptance for his project in accordance with the Plumbing Code, the Elevator Code, the Electrical Code, and FHA Rehabilitations Standards. Finally, after compliance with all of the requirements of these agencies, the architect must secure final approval of his plans and specifications from the Department of Sewers, the Department of Highways, the Department of Taxation and the Department of Air Pollution. A permit to build may then be granted. The cost of these bureaucratic hassles will ultimately be passed on to the consumer.

Of the 3,000 counties in the U.S., less than one-half have any form whatever of building code regulation.[1] When one chooses a specific area for a homeplace, a move of a few miles into an adjacent county may represent a saving of $2,000 or more in building costs. It is important to the prospective homebuilder to find out from local county government the present and the projected status of code enforcement in that area. It is important for a homebuilder to know, for instance, that Oregon, California, Indiana, North Carolina, Ohio, Wisconsin, Michigan, Montana, New Mexico and Washington have, at this writing, mandatory

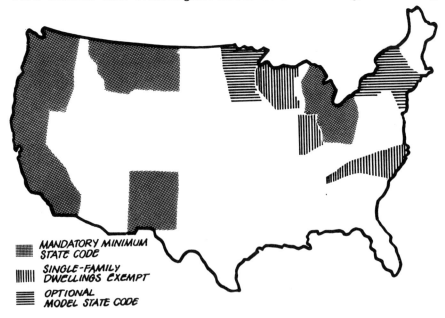

MANDATORY MINIMUM
STATE CODE

SINGLE-FAMILY
DWELLINGS EXEMPT

OPTIONAL
MODEL STATE CODE

state-wide building code ordinances.[2] Some state codes, however, exempt farm buildings, while other codes, like those in the states of Indiana, North Carolina and Wisconsin, do not include under their regulation singe-family dwellings. Possibly the most stringent, all-powerful code enforcement takes place in California. Paradoxically, it is in California—perhaps more than in any other state— that the low-income, marginal owner-builder seeks to settle and build. People gravitating to this state are deceived to think that, even in the sparsely-settled mountain communtiies, there will be personal freedom and opportunity for them to build. On the contrary, there is not one spot in the entire state, however isolated, which is exempt from the Uniform Building Code.

A number of books on the subject of buying country property have appeared in recent years. Authors of these books list climate conditions, land cost and taxes, and community amenities as the more important factors influencing one's choice of location for building. Seldom when consulting these books does one find that

Philip and his wife bought land in a code-enforced area but were unable to obtain a building permit because of pending sub-division litigation. They built anyway—keeping photographic records to prove they had built to code.

these writers examine the ramifications of zoning and building regulation's on one's purchase. These regulations may, however, determine whether it is at all feasible for one to build a homeplace anywhere.

A sum of $1,500 is customarily assumed by commercial builders to be the average, additional amount required to build a house in code-enforced areas. More specifically, total costs of identical houses in two, similar northern Illinois towns were recently calculated. Code requirements in one community raised the building costs $2,000 above the costs of building in the other community. When this additional cost was carried by the home-owner over the full term of the mortgage payments (30 years at 7% interest), monthly payments were increased by $13.31. Based on the custom of allocating 25% of one's budget for housing, an additional $640 of annual income would be required to qualify the owner of one of these homes for a mortgage. The final cost of the house would total an additional $4,790.

The National Association of Home Builders has estimated that each $1,000 reduction in the price of a new house would enable an additional 75,000 families to become eligible to purchase needed housing. Presently, two-thirds of the population of this country does not earn enough money to afford the lowest priced, minimal— but code-enforced—new housing.

Why would a house which is built to code cost hundreds and even thousands of dollars more? In the 1920s, Secretary of Commerce, Herbert Hoover, advised Congress that 10% of all building costs—from foundation to roof—would be saved by eliminating conflicting, out-dated elements of building codes. In more recent years, the National Commission on Urban Problems raised this estimate to be a saving of 15% on all building costs for home builders. The Commission lists many "excessive code requirements" which, in 1969, added $1,838 to the cost of a $12,000 house of 1,000 square feet. Some of these important items are listed below:

FREQUENT CODE REQUIREMENTS AND THEIR COSTS [3]

1. Foundations dug to clay when piers and grade
beam would do as well...$150
2. Extra number and sizing of joists....................................... 63
3. 2x4 studs supporting outside walls 16" o.c.
when 24" o.c. entirely adequate... 125

4. Extra sheathing 125
5. Separate siding and sheathing instead of
   single 3/8" panel.. 330
6. Double framed 2x4s for window and door openings
   although single 2x4s considered sufficient........................... 40
7. Each door and window must have own header
   when continuous double 2x6 atop outside wall is
   better... 45
8. Extra door and window headers... 20
9. Extra fire wall requirements in frame construction............. 50
10. Interior walls 4" thick even though
    2" walls safe when non-load bearing................................. 310
11. Subfloor must be 3/4" instead of 1/2" plywood.................. 500
12. Double 2x4 plate on all wall partitions
    where single member sufficient.. 30
13. Trusses on 16" centers where 24" centers
    sufficient.. 100
14. Masonry chimney when Class B flue would do
    a better job... 150
15. Extra electric over National Electric Code
    when rigid conduit required... 300
16. Metal conduit required for wiring when Romex
    (non-metallic sheathed cable) just as good........................ 200
17. All electrical wiring to be accomplished by
    a licensed electrician.. 100
18. All plumbing, drainage, waste and vent size
    must be 2" minimum.. 30
19. Install lead pan under all shower bases
    regardless of type instead of other means
    of water protection... 50
20. Central cold air return cannot be used
    in heating. Each room must have its
    own air return to furnace.. 85

Not included in the Commission report were alternative building methods and materials which, if permitted, would provide even greater savings. Builders may save $300, for example, on the cost of a $30,000 construction if they are not required to form the foundation footing with wood. A simple trench footing performs satisfactorily and provides equivalent strength. A survey by the National Association of Home Builders of 1,200 communities indicates that the code prohibits half of them from using a concrete post and grade beam foundation. Using a 2-inch, non-bearing partition wall saves $400 in an average-size house, but code requires *all* walls to be 4-inches thick.

Industry must assume responsibility for added building costs

This 784 sq. ft. non-code house was built (without running water and using much salvaged material) for $1.30 per square foot in 1972.

through the influence it exerts in its special-interest-support of the code. Representatives of the cast iron industry, for example, wage a relentless battle against their competitors, the plastic pipe industry. One result of this unremitting rivalry is found in the code stipulation of the City of Pittsburgh, which requires 400% more vent piping in bathrooms than is specified by the National Plumbing Code. Today, three-fourths of the coded areas of the U.S. prohibit the use of plastic pipe in drainage systems. Such diverse groups as professional societies, insurance underwriters, lending institutions, trade associations, labor unions and contractor associations all have a special interest in influencing the code.

Government agencies also greatly influence code requirements. The USA Standards Institute, for example, has been influential in the regulation of masonry bearing wall design. One result is that a 25-story building in Canada may have 8-inch-thick, lock-brick bearing walls, but in this country, the same 25-story building would be required to have standard-brick walls 20-inches thick. Other examples of burgeoning government influence on building code requirements will be discussed in Chapter 14.

The National Commission on Urban Problems maintains that, "The increase in the cost of money has added more to the ultimate cost of a house than any other single item." A rise of a mere 1% interest on a $20,000 mortgage increases monthly payments by $15. Nowadays, it is not uncommon for people to pay 10% interest on money borrowed to build code-approved housing. Yet, bankers have openly testified in Congressional hearings that their total cost for providing a home mortgage is on the order of 1½%. The cost to the bank for making such a loan is only 0.30% of this total charge. Loan servicing and administrative expenses amount to 0.50%, and only 0.65% of the total is expended in determining the risk factor for bank losses through foreclosure.

In her classic study of American housing, Edith Elmer Wood had this to say about the money squeeze:

> The crux of the housing problem is economic. Under the ordinary laws of supply and demand, it is insoluble. In our modern industrial civilizations, the distribution of income is such that a substantial portion of the population cannot pay a commercial rent, much less a commercial price, for a home fulfilling the minimum health and decency requirements.[4]

One may take issue with some of Miss Wood's premises on the basis that they were written in 1931, but remember that banks today issue money for construction loans only on code-approved housing. It is rare, indeed, to find any lending institutions which will loan money to owner-builders, even if they meet code requirements and even if they build in a code-protected area. Generally, a bonded, licensed contractor must be legally committed to the project before institutionally loaned money is made available for a house building project.

The housing situation, alluded to by Miss Wood in 1931, was to have been "improved" in 1934 by the creation of the Federal Housing Administration (FHA). The original purpose for the creation of such an agency of government was to stabilize the lending situation for home builders by insuring mortgages and by allowing low down-payments on long-term mortgages. In actual practice, however, FHA has rarely functioned for the benefit of the house-needy in rural populations of less than 25,000. In fact, FHA has benefitted seven-times more middle and upper income groups desirous of housing than it has benefitted low and moderate income groups having acute housing needs.

FHA operates only in concert with code-enforced, contractor-built enterprise. From the "public housing" of the 1930's to the "mortgage assistance" of the 1970's, Federal Housing Assistance programs have been a joke. The two million federally-assisted housing units erected in its 34-year history are now required by the public every two years!

Clay Cochran, of the National Rural Housing Coalition, succinctly summed up the housing situation for the McGovern Select Committee on Nutrition and Human Needs when he said, "Congress apparently never intended that FHA should be anything except a scow on which lenders, realtors, developers, surveyors, title and finance companies, and the rest of the camp followers of the housing industry could ride when they could not get aboard the yacht operated by banks, insurance companies, savings and loan and other lenders catering to the better quality—that is, more affluent folk."

In discussion about the economic effects of code regulation on a person's ability to provide basic shelter needs, we must also consider the influence that building and zoning regulations have on land-use policies. The price of land is only partly inflated by unscrupulous speculators. Agencies of both government and the private sector of the economy also contribute to the artificial rise in land values. In 1954, Federal Urban Renewal (referred to by some as Negro Removal) was legislated by Congress and approved by the Supreme Court. This agency has the authority to forcibly seize the private property of any individual—after, of course, paying the individual the appraised value of the property—and convey it to another private individual. In the process, new and added code and zoning stipulations for occupancy are imposed upon the recipient. Furthermore, the 1970 report from the General Accounting Office states that $3\frac{1}{2}$-times as many housing units have been demolished through Urban Renewal as have been built by it. Less than half of those units which were subsequently rebuilt with government financing were for low and moderate income families.

Before federal subsidies are released to cities for renewal purposes, for public housing, or for revenue sharing, they must have functional building and zoning codes. At one time, the agency of Housing and Urgan Development impounded $35 million of Urban Renewal funds from the City of San Francisco. These funds were withheld until that city agreed to comply with the demand of the agency to up-date its building code. It did.

The code has become the great social leveler for the people of this country in their quest for housing. Vacated housing that has become distasteful to middle class occupants cannot—because of code restrictions—be legally occupied by low-income house holders. When George Romney, one-time Secretary of the Department of Housing and Urban Development, said that 80% of the American people cannot afford to buy new housing at 1970 prices, he was talking about code-regulated, bank-loan-approved, contractor-built housing.

Housing and building codes were enacted to protect nineteenth century tenement dwellers from the outrageous practices of landlords and slum builders. They are justifiably applied today in behalf of urban and suburban renters and unwitting home-buying consumers. The codes are difficult to justify, however, when one realizes that they have extended far beyond the original intent to protect the public health and safety. The code's ever-widening realm of control keeps housing beyond the financial reach of the majority of the people and makes outlaws of those who attempt to build their own less-expensive alternatives.

Since houseboats do not fit easily into existing building code classifications, they are usually one of the last types of dwelling to be regulated.

Dale and Martha's House

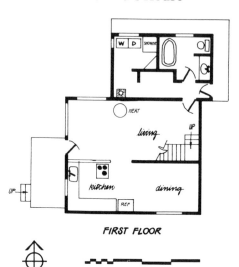

FIRST FLOOR

SECOND FLOOR

0   5   10   15   20 FT

cost . . . . unknown
sq. feet 1,356

Description

This two-story frame house has been built in two stages. The first part to be built, the 20'x24' section containing the kitchen, dining area, living room, and three bedrooms upstairs, was originally intended to be a garage. It has a concrete slab floor, walls of standard 2x4 frame construction sheathed with plywood, and a low (1" in 12") pitch roof. The smaller (11'x18') addition rests on a continuous concrete foundation supported by 18"x24" footings. The floor girders are cantilevered 30" on the first floor and 84" on the second floor to support the wooden walkway and deck shown in the plan. The framing of this addition differs from that of the original building only in that the second floor and roof are made of 2x6 tongue and groove hemlock on 4x8 joists and rafters, as opposed to the plywood on 2x6 scheme used in the original building.

All the windows in both sections are aluminum sliders. Water comes from an uphill spring but supplies only the kitchen sink, since the new bathroom and laundry have yet to be completed. There is a hand-made

septic system, but for now, the family uses an outhouse. The house is heated by electric baseboard heaters occasionally supplemented by a wood heater.

Comments

Six years ago, Dale, Martha, and their three children were living in town next to a public school. They disliked the noise of the school and were discouraged by the difficulty of achieving privacy. One too many balls bounced against the side of their house, and they decided to move out of town. Dale admits he "had no business" buying so much land on the wages he was earning as a warehouseman, but he was determined to provide his family with some privacy.

The first thing to be built was a garage—or so it was planned. Dale had never built a building before so he wanted his first attempt to be simple. Because of his limited budget, he wanted it to be useful. He built the garage with the idea that his family could live in it temporarily until a house could be built. That was six years ago. Dale and his famly (now increased to six members) have lived in this "garage" with no bathroom ever since. Dale hasn't been idle these six years; he has built a storage shed larger than the "garage," he has laid concrete walks between his buildings, and he has made his entire septic system by hand.

The reason he hasn't started building the house is that he and his family decided that the garage would make a perfectly adequate house if a few additions were made to it. Accordingly, he has set about constructing the two-story bathroom-laundry-bedroom addition now in progress. When this is complete, he has plans to remove the low-pitch roof over the garage portion of the building and replace it with a steeper double-pitch roof with a clerestory like the one shown in the elevation. He has further plans to expand the living room, to add an enclosed front porch, and to add a greenhouse.

NORTH ELEVATION

4. Failures

A close look at the UBC exposes it for more than mere verbosity. Ominous is the control vested in the state over construction *of any sort.* Many of the requirements pertaining to dwellings are of dubious relevance to the pledge of providing "minimum standards of safety, health, and welfare." While most of the world struggles to provide *any* type of housing for its people, in this country we place higher importance on codes of arbitrary standards than on housing itself. With 1975 industrial housing starts lagging 35% behind 1972,[1] self-made housing is an imperative to shelter provision for thousands of people.

The province of government over private construction is vast, as evidenced by the rythmically-worded Section 301 of the UBC:

> No person, firm, or corporation shall erect, construct, enlarge, alter, repair, move, improve, remove, convert, or demolish any building or structure in the city, or cause the same to be done, without first obtaining a separate building permit for each such building or structure from the Building Official.

The scope of authority of the building department indicates that the public is now being protected from itself as well as from professionals. The activities of an individual owner-builder are lumped together with those of industrial profiteers, despite their dissimilar motives and the different magnitude of their operations. "Alteration, repair, improvement, conversion, and demolition," performed by private individuals on their own property, seem to be overly broad regulatory concerns of government. The latter are common activities of many home owners who must obtain permits, pay fees, and seek the approval of the building official for even minor engagements in these domains.

O.C. Helton, a third-generation log cabin builder, attempted to get a permit to build a log house for himself, his wife and five children. When he realized that the required architect's drawings and engineer's stamp would cost him more than $1,000, he decided to go ahead without the permit. The county issued a stop-work-order and charged Helton with building without a permit. O.C. fought the charge claiming that the requirements for a building permit were, in his case, unreasonable. A jury of five men and a woman eventually found him innocent. "If you don't get this government slowed down and back to the people," he later said, "by the time my children want to build their home, they'll be surrounded by rules."

The historical failure of private industry to responsibly regulate itself has required government intervention. There is no historical equivalent of individuals failing themselves in the course of building for themselves when they are allowed proper choices. Yet, the code transfers the responsibility shirked by trade professionals to building department officials—while the public exchanges its freedom for "protection."

Objects, like activities, are broadly defined by the code. The code's definition of "structure" is:

> That which is built or constructed, an edifice or building of any kind, or piece of work artificially built up or composed of parts joined together in some definite manner. (Sec. 420)

This, too, is an all-inclusive provision which leaves virtually no room for creation of any form. An "edifice...composed of parts joined together" could mean anything from a doghouse to an art sculpture—or for that matter to a bicycle assembled from parts. Obviously, the code was not designed to regulate birdhouse production. The point is, the code is a sweeping piece of legislation which is so broad as to be vague and, in the grey area of interpretation, the possibilities for selective and arbitrary enforcement are real.

Ironically, in many cases rural owner-builders call upon building officials to use their discretionary powers to waive excessive code requirements which common sense deems ludicrous. Too often, however, officials will claim to have no authority in these situations, stating that they must hold to the letter of the law. This is not always the case, however, for some building officials will flexibly interpret the code to meet its "intent," thereby earning the respect and co-operation of the public.

Section 106 of the UBC allows a building official to use judgement in the approval of "alternative materials or designs," provided he finds the proposed design is satsfactory and in compliance with the engineering requirements of the code. Section 107, however, says that the official may "require tests as proof of compliance...if insufficient evidence" that the requirements are met is offered by the designer. Proof of compliance must be provided "at the expense of the owner." This often means that an owner-builder must hire an engineer or architect to supply computations as proof for the building official. The cost of engineering can actually exceed the cost of the house in the situation where salvaged materials are used.

Building departments justify their reluctance to approve alternative designs, even when construction modifications are slight, on the basis of their fear of potential liability. This seems an unwarranted fear, since Sec. 212g of the UBC waives personal liability for any employee charged with the enforcement of the code if he "acts in good faith...in the discharge of his duties." More likely, it is a lack of willingness to stray from the routine bureaucratic tasks which inhibit a building official in a moment of critical decision.

The distinction between rural and urban that owner-builders make in objecting to the codes is a reasonable one to draw. In fact, it is significant that public codes such as the UBC, specify that they apply "within the city." When counties adopt state-executed codes, they re-define "city" to mean "the county." This translation presupposes that urban and rural situations are equivalent, therefore the health and safety factors must likewise be equal. This is like prescribing a life jacket for a desert hiker, which is reasonable only if one equates the hazards of the ocean with those of the desert.

In the city people share sidewalks, streets, walls, stairways, and even lavatories. In the city, thousands of people may abide on one square acre. It is therefore logical that a narrower definition of safety be set for city builders. City construction directly affects the safety and sensibilities of scores of people. The authors believe, however, that even in the city, freedom to build for oneself should be maximized and set apart from construction motivated by profit.

When one looks at many of the dwelling requirements in the codes, one can easily surmise that they were intended to insure that corner-cutting professional builders would provide a uniform standard of basic amenities. For owner-builders, however, their standard is their own. Many of these requirements clearly fall within the realm of individual discretion when applied to people building their own houses.

For example, Section 1405a of the UBC states that "...a dwelling unit shall be provided with natural light by means of windows or skylights with an area of not less than one-tenth of the floor area of such rooms..." Section 1407a requires a ceiling height in habitable rooms of "not less than 7 feet 6 inches." Section 1407b calls for every dwelling unit to have "at least one room which shall have not less than 150 square feet of floor area."

Section H 503b of the Uniform Housing Code (UHC) embellishes these requirements by demanding that living units have "a living room of not less than 220 square feet of superficial floor area. An additional 100 square feet...shall be provided for each occupant in excess of two."

It is the reasonable contention of many owner-builders that floor and window space should be a matter of choice in one's own home. It is doubtful that an owner-builder would fail to provide adequate windows or floor space and, if this happened, living in the house would spur amendment to the original design. Is it logically the

Common sense enables owner-builders to provide adequate window area. Is it logically the province of government to dictate the numbers and sizes of windows in one's home?

province of the state to determine the size of a person's living room? One wonders if people would vote away their right to determine their own room dimensions—or if they even know they have *already* lost this right!

In these times of "energy crisis," the UBC (Sec. 1410) and the UHC (Sec. H 701a) require "heating facilities capable of maintaining a room temperature of 70 degrees F. at a point 3 feet above the floor in all habitable rooms." This clause excludes wood heating as an adequate method because, in the words of one building official, "...a BTU rating cannot be established for wood heat."

Rural owner-builders employ wood heaters as their *only* source of heat, and for this they are often held in violation by building inspectors. Wood is a readily available fuel in many rural environments, and its utilization does not contribute to the depletion of fossil fuels. Indeed, much available country land has already been logged by timber companies and the remaining fire-hazardous slash provides fine wood heat. Instead of being commended for using a resourceful alternative to consumptive heating devices or for clearing slash, owner-builders may find abatement proceedings against their houses for "lack of adequate heating facilities."

Many owner-builders find automated water systems costly and wasteful of energy. Section H 505d of the UHC says:

> All plumbing fixtures shall be connected to an approved system of water supply and be provided with hot and cold running water, except water closets shall be provided with cold water only.

Owner-builders often own land where their water source is lower in elevation than logical building sites, thus preventing gravity-fed running water systems. Hand pumps are time-proven instruments of water delivery, but they are not acceptable by virtue of this code provision. In addition, to haul one's water manually is illegal. Hauling water is a tedious but joyous task for many owner-builders, although this activity is usually performed on a temporary basis. Water carriers, by being so directly involved in the process of the water's delivery, often gain a great appreciation for this precious element. In a culture so disrespectful of water, we feel this experience can be a healthy one.

Hot and cold running water is a nice convenience but not demonstrably necessary for health and safety. In winter months, rural dwellers often heat water on their wood stoves, either in pots on the stove or with a plumbing system piped through the stove. In summer months, exterior coiled pipes capture solar heat to produce hot water during the warm hours of the day. These systems are energy conserving but are not "up to code," because hot water only occurs when the sun is high or when the stove is stoked.

The code expects all dwelling units to be replete with all amenities before it is inhabited. It is the assumption of the code that dwellings will be provided by professionals for other people's use. It must be remembered that owner-built projects are living experiences which grow gradually and organically. Owner-builders fully expect to provide themselves with all of the comforts of home, but over a period of time.

Section H 701a of the UHC makes electricity a dwelling requirement where "...power is available within 300' of the premises." Electricity is certainly not a necessity of life, and many rural owner-builders prefer to live without it. Urban culture, with its

Expensive engineering tests would be required to build this Cinva Ram earth block house to code. Rick, however, never intended to get a permit since his immediate plans did not include such items as a full bathroom, required by the code. He built this 600 sq. ft. house without a permit for $900.

wasteful electrical consumer gadgets—can openers, hair dryers, toothbrushes, etc.—uneasily moves toward power rationing, yet the codes require electricity for those who don't want it!

Electricity and the previous examples of room dimensions, plumbing requirements, and heating systems prescribed by the code as "safety factors" are *conveniences* only, not prerequisites to health and safety. Owner-builders assert that they are capable of defining their own conveniences. Unfortunately, however, failure to conform with the code's definition of "adequacy" may lead to a $300 fine and/or 90 days in jail (Sec. 205 of the UBC) or, worse yet, to actual demolition of the "nuisance" building. Carl Jung's words are again relevant to the owner-builder's case:

> I have done without electricity, and tend the fireplace and stove myself. Evenings, I light the old lamps. There is no running water, and I pump the water from the well. I chop the wood and cook the food. These simple acts make man simple; and how difficult it is to be simple!

The plan-as-you-go approach to building is made problematical by the UBC. Section 302a states that "approved plans and specifi-

This owner-built house was under construction for ten years. All the beams and the doors are hand-hewn. In an attempt to emulate thatch, enough composition roofing for 15 normal houses was used. When snoopers destroyed their privacy, the owners were forced to sell—only eight years after the house was completed. It is now a tourist attraction.

cations shall not be changed, modified, or altered without authorization from the Building Official, and all work shall be done in accordance with the approved plans." Section 313b further states that, "Where plans...are changed, as to require additional plan checking, an additional plan check fee shall be charged." Building department plan checking can be notoriously slow, which means that a suspension in building momentum is created when plans are altered. Not only do these provisions rob the home building project of spontaneity, but they force the builder to pay for plan modification as well.

There is a Catch-22 quality to the codes in that abatement is precipitated by failure to comply with code specifications, rather than for any actual harm to the public health or safety. It is one thing to specify that a rock wall must be so many inches thick and another to state that a rock wall must be able to sustain the load required of it. The code is a shopping list of arbitrary *specifications*, materials, and designs, not a helpful guide to *performance*

Dozens of 55 gallon drums and a system of vertical "gin poles" allow Leo Smith's house to rise and fall with the seasonal high water near the river.

standards. It fails to mention pier, pole or pile foundations, post and beam construction, log cabins, loft ladders, owner-constructed sinks or tubs, and many other materials and methods commonly used by owner-builders. Each of these deviations requires computations by a registered engineer or architect. The fact that lumber must be "graded by an approved agency" (Sec. 2505 UBC) means that home-milled or recycled lumber, hand-hewn beams, and hand-split shakes can only be used if inspected by a certified grader. The owner-builder must pay a high hourly rate, plus portal-to-portal mileage to the grader. This cost may exceed the cost of the lumber! In instances where the building department assigns a grade itself, by policy it assigns a low grade, even if heartwood is being considered.

There are other omissions to the building codes also questionable to owner-builders. For instance, there is no provision for temporary dwellings of limited life span. The code allows only a "material or method of construction that is *permanent*." (UBC, Vol. 6, Introduction) This principal is, of course, limited. Nobody is expected to equal the architectural endurance record of the pyramids. Owner-builders will often build an initial structure for immediate shelter, while plans are developed and material gathered for a "permanent" house.

There is no provision in the code for construction of bedrooms or other living spaces detached from, but in conjunction with, a main structure harboring kitchen and sanitation facilities. Every building for habitation is expected to be a complete code unit, meeting all of the dwelling requirements. It is often desirable to have a bedroom, tea room, or study detached from the activity of the main house.

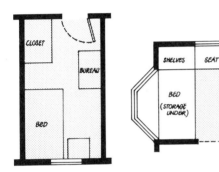

A poorly designed bedroom with the minimum "superficial floor area" allowed by the code compared to a bedroom with one sixth the allowable area.

The assumption that building to code is equal to the only acceptable standard of safety is contradicted by the fact that pre-code buildings are exempted from it. If the code is the absolute formula for safety, then what about all of the enduring buildings erected prior to its passage? Why are they not required to be brought up to code? One answer is that federal laws prohibit the enactment of retroactive laws. Another is that (a) people would rebel against the costly imposition of having to "improve" what has already been built, because (b) it is a myth that health and safety occur only when sanctioned by code prescription.

An example comes to mind of three owner-builders in a rural, Northern California county who were ordered to tear down their "substandard" homes. They had been cited for typical housing code violations—lack of proper water closet, lack of adequate heating facilities, room dimensions less than those required by the code, etc. Rather than pay the expense of having the county do it, they dismantled the homes themselves. The three, knowing that demolition of their homes was inevitable, had lived under psychological duress during the year-long abatement proceedings against them. Even the local building inspector conceded that the houses, though tacky in appearance, were warm and cozy quarters inside. The destruction of their homes put an end to their homestead development and virtually ruined them economically. Ultimately, they were forced to move into a rat-infested apartment building in the city. The rent was exorbitant, as city rates often are, and the creaky building was a far cry from the comfort they had known in their former homes, which were vermin-free. The letter of the code had been served, but had justice?

Perhaps the biggest failure of the uniform codes is the procedure by which they become law. Every three years, state legislatures perfunctorily adopt the codes into law *by reference*, based on the trusted know-how of the authors—the various conferences of building officials. These quasi-legislative authorities write the codes with no lay input. Public consent comes very indirectly through the elected legislators who, because of the code's technicality, rarely read them. It is a closed system smacking of vested interest. As one commentator noted:

> With some notable exceptions, people concerned about the future supply and cost of new housing in the United States lament the fact that local building codes, in seeking to protect the public health and safety, also discourage innovation. The dissenters are skilled workers, traditional material suppliers, and local building officials, whose jobs, businesses, and functions depend on doing things the traditional way. Given such dependence, their attitudes are natural and typical reactions of established interests vulnerable to technological change, who seek shelter from competition in the high purpose of public regulation.[2]

Democratic procedure is short-circuited within the code framework. Appeals against any notice, order, or action by the building official are made to a Board of Appeals, of which the official is an *ex-officio* member. The other members are generally contractors or engineers. Rarely is there any lay representation on the Board of Appeals.

All told, the uniform codes are a riddle to everyone involved with them, except perhaps, their authors. Legislators allow a select group of professionals to write the codes, and inspectors enforce the provisions of these laws, often without understanding the engineering and detailed regulations included in the text. Building officials are wary of using their better judgement for fear of public outcries of selective enforcement. The cost of housing rises in code-enforced jurisdictions, and people are forced to play a cat-and-mouse game with inspectors.

People who build for their own use—owner-builders—are left out in the cold, because the code is not geared to incorporate their reality into its provisions. They fall under the same blanket of regulations as the professionals. Uniform codes for all is a myth, for circumstances are rarely uniform. Codes are no more egalitarian than tax laws. They tell you what you must do, not what you can't. This precludes creative alternatives to the given, "uniform" model. As one owner-builder explained to a rural Grand Jury when testifying why he is an "outlaw" builder: "I never bought a permit, because there weren't any for sale for what I wanted to do!"

Jane's Double Rhombic Dodecahedron

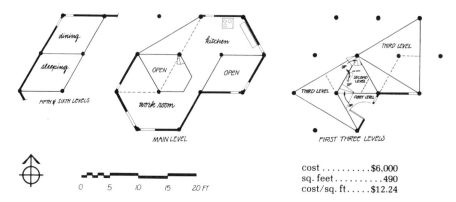

dining

sleeping

FIFTH & SIXTH LEVELS

kitchen

OPEN

OPEN

work room

MAIN LEVEL

THIRD LEVEL

SECOND LEVEL

THIRD LEVEL

FIRST LEVEL

UP

FIRST THREE LEVELS

0   5   10   15   20 FT

cost $6,000
sq. feet 490
cost/sq. ft $12.24

Description

Inside this structure there are six levels, each approximately 30" above the previous one. The first three levels are devoted to entry and storage. One enters at the first level and ascends a collection of built-in stairs and movable stumps to the fourth (main) level, containing kitchen and workroom. The fifth level is a dining room, and the sixth a sleeping loft.

The structure is built on 14 spruce poles. Each pole is creosoted and anchored five feet into the ground. The floors are made of 2x6 joists covered with ½" plywood and oak flooring. The 2x4 walls are covered on the outside with ship-lapped 1x6 spruce. The 2x10 rafters are covered with plywood and 90 lb. rolled roofing.

There is 8½" of fiberglass insulation in the ceiling, 3½" in the walls, and 6" over the sloping canvas

skirts. The space is heated with a wood heater. The house is wired, but there is no running water. There is an open-air outhouse. With the exception of the windows and oak flooring, all materials were purchased new.

Comments

Jane was drafting in a San Francisco architect's office when she became interested in pre-fabrication. H.U.D.'s modular housing competition had just been announced, and Jane had started to think about close-packing systems that would fit into a triangular grid. She discovered rhombic dodecahedrons and liked them because all the rhombic panels could be identical. "It was a good year for panels and pre-fab ideas," she says.

She spent the following year building cardboard models and studying regular geometry. She decided to actually build the house she had designed because she wanted to test her pre-fab ideas at full scale. She also wondered what it would be like to live in a rhombic dodecahedron. She bought five acres near Fairbanks, Alaska, and she arranged to hire a neighbor to help with the framing.

At the time the poles were being set into the ground, the house was to be a framework of 2x8's, covered with burlap and sprayed with urethane foam. All the pieces were going to be pre-cut. Once the poles were set, however, Jane discovered that they had not been placed as precisely as she had planned. Everything would have to be fitted piece-by-piece. All the precise figuring on paper went down the drain.

As she was building the floors, Jane began to have second thoughts about spraying the building with foam. Foam must be sprayed on a warm day, and the weather was already turning cooler. She talked to a number of people who were having problems with foam domes. She also did some cost estimating at this point, and, when she discovered how much less it would cost to enclose the house with conventional materials, she abandoned the idea of using foam. "The whole house was built this haphazardly," she says.

Jane did enclose the house before winter, and she feels her overall effort was successful. She enjoys the spaces and says that living in the house suits her very well. Her principle regret is that she didn't spend more effort to insure that the place could be heated in the winter—there is too much glass and there are too many air leaks. "In Alaska," she says, "heat should be the first consideration, not the last."

5. Safe and Sanitary

It is difficult to modify building codes, but impossible to alter the status quo in the realm of sanitation. A building, at least, can be stress-tested for safety or intelligently inspected on the site. In approaching the sanitation establishment, however, one encounters the full force of germ mythology in which one is led to believe that a ceramic toilet is somehow organically connected to the excretion process itself. One wonders how man arrived in the Twentieth Century without the benefit of Thomas Crapper's water closet.

We do not mean to be flippant about the serious matter of excreta disposal for, indeed, enteric disease is the principal cause of death in many countries. But we do not subscribe to the Western cleanliness fetish, which fosters a totally irrational approach to basic biological functions. Before launching into a critique of "approved" sanitation systems, we must mention that this chapter is relevant to the subject of building one's home. At least half of the owner-builders hassled by authorities are cited for building unapproved sewage systems. A look at the sanitation requirements of the UBC should illustrate why this is so:

> Every dwelling unit shall be provided with a kitchen sink and with bathroom facilities consisting of a water closet, lavatory and either a bathtub or shower. Plumbing fixtures shall be provided with running water necessary for their operation.

Rural owner-builders, who are blessed with ample space to engage their design fantasies, often create bathing facilities detached from the main living quarters. Saunas and bath houses, in the style of Scandanavian and Oriental nations, are popular alternatives. These facilities are illegal, but stand a reasonable chance

*This pit privy has been serv-
ing a family of four whose
code-approved septic system
failed because of poor soil
conditions.*

of being negotiated with local authorities. The big stumbling block
is the requirement for sewage treatment.

In accordance with the procedure in most code-enforced jurisdictions, a building permit will not be issued unless a sewage
permit has first been granted by the local health department. The
commonly accepted sanitation schemes are the community sewer
and the septic-tank-leach-field systems. Being limited to these two
systems precludes the common homestead methods of excreta
disposal—the pit privy (outhouse) and the compost privy. This
limitation adds greatly to construction costs, is often unworkable
and, in the case of community sewage systems, is an ecological
disaster.

Community sewage installations are curious affairs. A ceramic
bowl is connected to miles of pipe which transport one part excreta
in 100 parts of clean water to a central treatment plant. Billions of
dollars are spent trying to separate the two. The effluent is
dumped into the nearest body of water where it feeds algae which
rapidly reproduce, consuming oxygen and thereby destroying
aquatic life. Meanwhile, soil is deprived of the benefits of human
fertilizer, and other organic matter is drained into the sewer.

The April, 1975 issue of *Smithsonian* magazine ran an article entitled, "An Idea in Need of Re-thinking: The Flush Toilet," by Sam Love, who lucidly examines the social cost of contemporary sewage systems. Love points out that they are the direct descendants of cess pits and open sewers which emptied into rivers. Water, as a waste-removal vehicle, was satisfactory to the urban user who no longer had to contend with a mess on city streets, but this arrangement was not so satisfactory to downstream residents. Today, virtually everyone is downstream from someone else. The effect of unconsciously dumping human waste into our waterways—"wastes" of the flush-and-forget culture, including disposable diapers, razor blades, tampax, photographic chemicals and scores of other unbiodegradables—will be a serious problem for future generations.

Love estimates that in one year the average North American family uses 35,200 gallons of water for flushing alone. The energy costs of large centralized sewage treatment plants are even more staggering:

> ...one estimate is that, at full capacity, a 309 million-gallons-a-day waste-treatment system, such as that being built in Washington, D.C., will consume as much as 900,000 kilowatt hours of electricity, 500 tons of chemicals and 45,000 gallons of fuel oil daily.[1]

For the ecology-minded owner-builder, it is impossible to justify using a community sewer system. In rural areas, however, these systems rarely exist, but the other choice can have its drawbacks. We can be kinder with a critique of the septic tank except that it, too, employs water as the vehicle for removal of waste. Many owner-builders do not have enough water to afford the five-gallon-flush, even if they are so inclined. Where the water table rises near the surface in the rainy season, septic tanks are rendered useless (and dangerous). Another criticism of the septic tank is that it is costly to build. In many cases, the cost of an approved septic tank exceeds the cost of an illegal home.

It is ironic that water-borne methods are the acceptable systems of waste removal, for water plays a predominant role in the transmission of certain enteric bacterial infections—typhoid and paratyphoid fevers, bacillary dysentery, and cholera, for example. It has an indirect relationship in the transmission of malaria. To prevent the proliferation of these bacteria, septic systems must be water-tight; hence, the costly pipes and tanks.

The idea of using human excrement for agricultural fertilizer is not new. In the Orient, a more mature attitude toward human waste has prevailed. For centuries, "night soil" has been diligently collected to fertilize fields. In Japan, the apartment rent of poor people may be paid in exchange for their sewage. In the country-side, farmers vie for the excrement of passing travelers by building attractive roadside outhouses.

The compost privy is a Western adaptation of the haul-it-away methods of the Orientals. It is utilized in the socially-progressive Scandanavian countries, and has been approved for use by the World Health Organization. Many investigations, including one conducted by the Swedish Health Ministry, have determined that harmful pathogens and worm eggs are unable to survive the temperature conditions and the biological antagonisms prevailing during the compost process. Rich humus is produced by adding organic matter to a chamber containing excrement. The compost privy does not operate on the questionable principal of using a

A compost privy built off the porch of a temporary dwelling. The permanent house was later built around this structure. One door leads to the in-use chamber, the other to the resting chamber. Rich humus taken from the privy is used to grow animal feed.

large amount of water to remove a small amount of bodily waste.

Compost privies are now on the market, and if the impassioned appeals of owner-builders cannot legalize them, commercialization probably will. The Clivus Multrum privy, developed in the late 1930s in Sweden, requires neither electricity nor chemicals and, with the addition of organic matter to the breakdown process, it produces utilizable compost. In the United States, a company established by Abby Rockefeller, Clivus Multrum USA, Inc., is now producing these composting toilets. The State of Maine has modified its plumbing code to permit their installation. A number of less-expensive compost privies have been developed which can be built by the layperson for as little as $100. A state Ad Hoc Sanitation Committee in California is studying compost privies to make recommendations as to their acceptability.

Pit privies or outhouses are found in most state parks and recreation areas, but are not permissable for dwellings except in "backward" localities. Even when one lives a distance away from the nearest neighbor, time-proven outhouses are usually taboo on a permanent basis. The World Health Organization, in a publication called "Excreta Disposal for Rural Areas and Small Communities," praises the pit privy as the best system for rural areas. Its advantages, enumerated are:

> 1) There is no soil or surface water pollution when the construction site is well-chosen;
> 2) It requires no attention or excreta handling;
> 3) Excreta will not be accessible to flies if the hole is kept covered, since flies shun dark holes and surfaces;
> 4) Odors are negligible and feces are out of sight;
> 5) The pit privy is simple in design, easy to use, does not require operation, and is inexpensive to build;
> 6) A rural family can build it with a minimum amount of assistance, with locally available materials;
> 7) Pathogenic bacteria do not usually find the soil a suitable environment for their multiplication.

The World Health Organization directs its research toward underdeveloped countries, but the United States should not be too proud to welcome information which could improve its domestic sanitation situation. An argument encountered by owner-builders at local health departments is that the pit privy is a "step backward." This is a difficult notion to dispell, because it reflects a cultural elitism which regulates outhouses to a lesser place in the "civilized" order. It is a significantly unscientific argument.

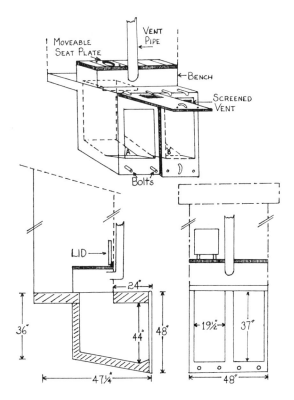

MOVEABLE
SEAT PLATE

VENT
PIPE

←BENCH

SCREENED
VENT

A

Bolts

LID→

24"

36"

44"

48"

19½"

37"

47¼"

48"

The prototype of the two-chamber D.S. Special composting privy, drawn above. State monitored tests of this system are in progress.

Even if local sanitarians intellectually agree with the principals of privies, it is beyond the scope of their authority to approve them. The functions of local health departments are multifaceted but, in the area of sewage disposal, their purpose is largely bureaucratic—to administer state guidelines. Alternatives must be approved by the massive state health bureaucracy before local departments will sanction them. Centralization thus robs local jurisdictions of the ability to solve the problems unique to their area and denies citizens the service they require.

In this regard, we can benefit from the World Health Organization's advice to rural sanitarians and public health officers: "You should strive to propose and design solutions that are within the means and ability of people to operate, maintain and replace."[2] In lieu of a willingness to provide these solutions, sanitary engineers merely become bureaucratic policemen. Rules are enumerated and compliance demanded. The result of this posture is that owner-builders learn they cannot depend on intelligent guidance from the guardians of public health. In the less accessible rural areas, many build illegal sewage systems.

Approved sewage systems may often be ruled out by local factors. Some of these include the soil type, the proximity of building sites to water sources, seasonal water shortage, high water tables, the slope of the land, the costliness of sanctioned systems, and a desire to recycle wastes. In the absence of official assistance, owner-builders will make critical decisions for themselves. The danger of this practice is obvious. In an effort to provide safe sanitation, their uneducated attempts may actually create health-hazardous situations for themselves and their community.

To sanitation engineers, the though of people building their own homes is somewhat debatable, but the thought of people building their own sanitation systems is terrifying. This is a justifiable fear, but as long as health departments remain unresponsive to people's needs, illegal sewage systems (like illegal homes) will be built without the blessing or the guidance of public experts. In the absence of public service, people are necessarily left to their own devices.

Fred's Plydome

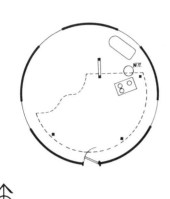

EAST ELEVATION

```
cost . . . . . . . . . . $300
sq. feet . . . . . . . . . 575
cost/sq. ft . . . . . . $0.52
```

```
0    5    10    15    20 FT
```

Description

This is a 24 foot plydome built from plans found in *Domebook I.* The basic structure consists of 30 sheets of 3/8" plywood bolted together to form a dome with pentagonal openings. The openings are covered with 10 mil vinyl to form windows. The plywood is covered with tarpaper and shingled with #4 (shim) shingles. After the dome was built, the floor, made of economy grade 2x8 decking, was laid on a plastic moisture barrier which lays directly on the ground. The sleeping loft was added later.

Water comes from an uphill spring and flows into an old bathtub which serves for all washing needs— kitchen and body. The water is heated by an old-fashioned system which circulates water through the wood cook stove and stores the hot water in a tank adjacent to the stove. The cook stove serves not only for heating water and for cooking, but also for heating the house. The place is so compact that, despite the lack of insulation, the small stove is sufficient to heat the space even in the coldest weather. There is a latrine a short distance downhill.

Comments

Fred's dome was built on a friend's

lot within the Portland, Ore. city limits. Fred was going to build a house for his friend, and the dome was to be his temporary shelter while he got organized. He applied to the city for a permit to build the dome as a job shack, and the permit was granted. It took about two weeks to build the dome, and Fred moved in. By the time the plans to build his friend's house had fallen through, Fred had become very comfortable in his "temporary" shelter.

He has lived in his dome for over a year now, and he's just beginning to hear the complaints of the Planning Commission. Fred says, "This is the only place I've ever lived that I'm entirely satisfied with, and the Planning Commission says I can't live here. It's at least comforting to know they can't just come and personally tear it down." He plans on staying until he is forced to move, and, if and when this should happen, he figures he can disassemble the dome and move it with him. He is, in fact, presently thinking about applying to the city for a mobile home permit.

Section Two
The Owner-Builder

The following four chapters (along with the case histories) introduce the reader to the people we call owner-builders. Who are these people? And why and how are they building their own homes?

6. A Profile

The owner-built houses of today are only the vanguard of a wave of activity that will astonish even the building supply retailers preparing for it. Just as some people are beginning to demand natural foods free from pesticides and preservatives, and just as they are realizing the benefits of bicycle transportation, so are they beginning to realize the benefits of designing and building their own homes. We have yet to hear from a Rachel Carson or a Ralph Nader of the housing industry, but when we do, the impact will be tremendous; the shortcomings of factory produced and professionally executed housing will be made obvious.

The people who have made these discoveries for themselves and who are designing and building their own houses are as diverse a group as could be found in this country today. There are mill-workers, lawyers, students, drop-outs, teachers, and Texas cowboys. They are unique individuals representing every occupation, religion, and political persuasion, but they have one important notion in common—a dissatisfaction with the choice of housing offered them by the American housing industry. This dissatisfaction is primarily centered around two factors, 1.) the cost of buying or renting a house and 2.) the mundane design typical of most housing in this country.

Most owner-builders have never previously owned a house, nor have they ever possessed the means to buy one in the conventional way. The frustration of paying rent is what prompts most of these people to begin thinking about owning their own house. But the thought of being tied down to regular house payments, spanning a period of 20 to 30 years, is often equally distasteful. For most

Owner-built homes are more prevalent than most people realize. This one is on a tyical 1.5 mile long rural road. A census of homes on the road showed 12 owner-built homes, no contractor-built homes, nine mobile homes, and one teepee. Many of the families living in mobile homes plan to build soon.

people, the only alternative to paying rent or mortgage is to build their own house, paying for it slowly, as it is built.

The other main area of dissatisfaction, the design of the typical American house, seems as important as financial considerations in prompting people to look elsewhere for their housing needs. The words "ticky-tacky," "little boxes," and "plastic" are used most frequently to describe their reactions. Owner-builders react not only against the repetition and lack of detail promoted by the discipline of mass-production and the rigid restrictions of the building codes, but they also react against the inclusion of "amenities" they would rather not have and for which they certainly do not want to pay. Some owner-builders do not need or want the minimum two bedrooms required by the FHA; some would rather do without electricity, would replace expensive heating systems with a pot-belly stove, or would replace the toilet with an outhouse.

Of course, the question of why owner-builders decide to start building their own houses is only partly answered by these dissatisfactions. The other part of the answer comes from the gratification they anticipate from designing and building their own houses. They imagine being able to have a house of any shape they want—designed by themselves to meet their most practical needs and their most whimsical fancies. They wonder what it would be like if no one else made these decisions for them. What would it be like to be an artist-house-builder in the only true sense—in a way that architects, who interpret clients' visions, and builders, who are allowed no visions at all, cannot? What would it be like to touch all the materials, to learn about placing them one against another? What would it be like if the mistakes were made by their own hands, instead of by the mechanisms of technology? What would it be like to have stories to tell about the creation of their houses? These are exciting questions which each person can answer only by proceeding with the design and construction of a home.

Most owner-built houses are located in a rural setting. It is tempting to blame the higher land costs and stricter building codes in urban areas for this phenomenon, but this is only part of the story. Even the occasional owner-built house found within urban boundaries is usually located in the most secluded and forested parts of the city. When questioned about their motives for choosing a rural setting, a large percentage of owner-builders mention a desire to "get out of the city" or to "get close to nature." It is curious that many of these people have never lived in a rural area before.

The forms of the houses being built by today's owner-builders are as diverse and as varied as the personalities of the owner-builders themselves. Still, there is a consistency of form running through them that cannot be ignored. They generally consist of simple shapes; they are built with many of the customary construction methods, and the conveniences, when they are included, are the standard ones typical of the average American house. The reasons for this consistency can be found in the same factors to which a consistency of house form is attributed in other cultures. These factors are: 1) climate, 2) the availability of materials, 3) the capabilities of the builder, and 4) the traditions of the society.[1]

CLIMATE The climate is temperate but not uniform in the region inhabited by most of the people included in this book—the region between the coast and the mountain ranges from northern California to the Canadian border. Average yearly rainfall increases (from 12"/year to 120"/year) and temperature decreases (20°F. design temperature difference) as one proceeds northward. As a result of these climatic differences, the owner-built houses of northern portions of the region favor orientation toward the sun and protection from the rain and cold to a greater degree than those of the southern portions. On the other hand, owner-built houses exist in the northern-most locations which compare almost identically to owner-built house in the most southerly locations. While climate does seem to play a role in determining the form of owner-built houses, this role seems to be a relatively minor one when compared with the following influences.

AVAILABILITY OF MATERIALS The quantity and variety of building materials available in this country at the present time would surpass the needs of the most eccentric owner-builder. Never before have people had such a wide array of building materials at their disposal. Of course, we are not dealing here with people who can afford to be eccentric. The need to keep the cost of materials as low as possible is an important priority in the minds of most owner-builders. This need considerably restricts the choice of

A young contractor who has built more than 20 houses in the area is building this house for his family.

available materials. In practical terms, it has meant that owner-builders have been restricted to salvaged materials and to new materials at the lower end of the price scale. The salvagable materials generally available to owner-builders are the easily extractable pieces of buildings from the past—windows, doors, fixtures, and lumber. The least expensive new materials tend to be the very ones used by contractors to build tract houses. Even if the use of these low-cost materials goes against their wishes, as it often does, owner-builder are compelled to use these materials they can afford.

Two-by-four lumber is the least expensive lumber suitable for structural support. The best low-cost insulation is designed to fit between two-by-four studs. It is the availability and the low cost of materials used in stud walls which make this type of construction so prevalent among owner-builders. The widespread use of these materials (and consequently of this type of construction) has a strong unifying effect on the form of owner-built houses.

CAPABILITIES OF BUILDER   The capabilities of the builder influence the form of houses in every culture. Owner-builders, of course, are a polymorphous group. Having come from very diverse backgrounds, they have acquired very different capabilities. In terms of their capabilities, in fact, the only thing owner-builders seem to share is a lack of experience in the area of construction. This inexperience contributes most significantly to a consistency of form in owner-built houses. It prompts most owner-builders to choose a simple design and a method of construction which has been tried and proven. This tendency promotes the use of the two-by-four frame construction employed by most contractors.

By using these commonplace methods and materials, inexperienced owner-builders are more able to acquire the instructions and guidance they will need to complete tasks which they have never before performed. There are many books available explaining two-by-four frame construction and the wiring, plumbing, etc., associated with it. Clerks in building supply outlets can usually explain how to install the parts they sell. For better or worse, two-by-four frame construction has become part of the collective experience of this culture. It is no coincidence that inexperienced owner-builders most frequently will choose to take advantage of this.

TRADITION   Tradition is another factor which tends to unify house form. Even after the climate, the materials, and the capabilities of the builder have influenced the house form, there are always a number of possible forms remaining. It is tradition that helps the builder make the final choice. A dramatic example of the effects of a strong tradition can be seen along the banks of the Nile River where houses built today are almost identical with houses built 4,000 years ago.

In the United States, where tradition has risen from a brief history of people from varied national and racial backgrounds, tradition is not as strong and therefore influences house form in a less dramatic way. The traditional American house is a single-family detached house, rectangular in plan, with a pitched roof, a fireplace, and separate rooms for cooking, dining, sleeping, and so forth. It can be built in a variety of ways while still conforming to the guidelines of this generalized traditional form.

The inability of American tradition to strictly define house form has allowed another form-defining factor to emerge. This is the factor of style, founded in the mood of the times as is fashion in clothing. The effects of style are much more short-lived than those of tradition. In this century alone, the traditional American house

Owner-builders enjoy the opportunity to express themselves, and traditional stylistic elements are frequently used for this purpose even when the house type is not of traditional origin.

has passed through the Victorian styles, the Bungalow style, and, more recently, the Ranch style. At present we seem to be emerging from the Ranch style and heading into what may be called the Barn style,[2] very much in evidence in many owner-built homes.

The owner-built projects described between the chapters of this book should illustrate the consistency of form discussed in the preceeding paragraphs as well as the diversity of form brought to each project by the unique personality of each owner-builder. These particular examples have been selected for their interest, and because we feel that they represent a cross-section of the houses we have seen. We hope that, collectively, they help the reader to form an overall impression of the process of building one's own home.

All plans are drawn to the same scale (1/16" = 1'0") and are oriented in approximately the same direction for easy comparison. So that the costs of construction may be compared, all cost figures are based on the finished house alone—without supporting systems such as roads, water, and septic systems. (Prospective owner-builders should realize that, depending on local conditions, these supporting systems can cost more than the house itself.) In cases where the house was incomplete at the time this data was collected (1972—1975), cost figures are based on the owners' best estimate of the cost of the completed house.

Robert's Studio

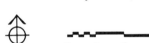

```
cost . . . . . . . . . $4,000
sq. feet . . . . . . . . . 592
cost/sq. ft . . . . . $6.76
```

```
0      5      10      15      20 FT
```

Description

This cruziform frame building sits on a west-sloping hillside of a 22 acre homestead, about 400 feet uphill from the original farmhouse. The main level contains a darkroom, a bathroom, and a studio/living space with a tiny kitchen in one corner. A ladder in the bathroom leads to the loft, with low-ceilinged nooks used for sleeping, drafting, and storage.

The building sits on pre-cast pier blocks arranged in a six-foot grid. Generously cross-braced 4x4 posts support the 2x6 floor joist system. The frame walls are sheathed on the exterior with 5/8" "reject" redwood plywood, insulated with fiberglass batts, and covered with ½" white fiberboard on the interior. The rafters are covered first with 1½" fiberboard insulation, followed by 1x4 nailing strips, 30 lb. felt, and split red cedar shakes. Near the top of each of the four roof facets is an openable plexiglass skylight. There is an oak floor on the main level. All windows and doors were made from scratch.

All materials were purchased new with the exception of the plumbing fixtures. Water is pumped up the hill from the old well next to the farmhouse. Sewage drains surreptitiously into a septic system recently installed for a future house. Electric baseboard heaters supplemented by a wood heat stove keep the place warm.

Comments

In August of 1972, after a year in Rome, Robert and Jessica returned to the small farmhouse Robert had bought just before they left. Robert is a film-maker and a designer and had been accustomed to a large space for his work. As they settled into their new surroundings, it became apparent that the farmhouse wasn't large enough to serve as both living space and working space. Realizing this, Robert designed a studio to accommodate his need for work space.

He had never constructed a building, so he hired an experienced carpenter to help with the framing. It took about a month to complete the shell of the building. Robert and Jessica took over from here—they

shingled the roof; made windows, doors, and skylights; wired; insulated; added interior paneling and trim; painted; and laid the floor. This took about six months.

By this time, they had decided that they could live in the studio and rent the farmhouse. Even though the studio was smaller than the farmhouse, they felt that, because it was more open (and thus more flexible), it could be organized to serve as both living and working space. The only apparent obstacle to this plan was the fact that the building permit for the studio specifically prohibited any plumbing (there was no septic tank). But the building had already passed the final framing and electrical inspections. There was no reason for building inspectors to return.

They added the plumbing (all but the water closet), and finally, nine months after the studio was begun, they moved in. Shortly thereafter, Robert enclosed a large space under the building for storage. About eight months later, Jessica left.

Since that time, Robert has added some cabinets, installed the water closet, and connected all the plumbing to a new septic system. Reflecting on the project, Robert feels that the space probably is too small for two people. As a house/studio for one person, however, he feels it is quite comfortable.

7. Design

The process of designing a house can be separated into three distinct phases: 1) the original considerations that are drawn into plans before construction begins, 2) the alterations of and additions to the original plans that take place during the course of construction, and 3) the continuous adjustments and changes that occur while the house is being used. Architects have traditionally concentrated on the completion of the first of these three phases for the purpose of minimizing the other two. Owner-builders, on the other hand, do a large portion of their design work during the second and third phases. They are able to do this because, unlike architects, owner-builders are not saddled with the responsibility of communicating their ideas to a builder before construction begins. Owner-builders are responsbile only to themselves, and thus they are able to spread their decisions over as long a period of time as they see fit, changing their minds as often as they please.

Since it is rare that owner-builders have much experience in either the design or construction of a house, they spend the bulk of the period prior to construction gathering information. They look for advice on the pros and cons of various construction methods, the costs of materials, the restrictions of the codes, and numerous other factors that will help them make decisions about the design of the house. Books are consulted, friends quizzed, building officials contacted, and building supply outlets pumped for prices and advice. Construction sites are visited and existing buildings are measured. Sometimes a practice project is undertaken.

As owner-builders are influenced by this newly-found information, their image of the house they want to build will grow,

A photographer is using the concepts found in Christopher Alexander's A Pattern Language *to help him design and build this house.*

sometimes slowly, sometimes rapidly, into a scheme about which they feel confident. This point of confidence is reached when the owner-builder has developed a firm conception of the shell of the house—its size, shape, cost, and basic structural system. The shell design lacks the exact details and dimensions needed to build the entire project, but it does include enough information to get started. It is a rough scheme, expected to be refined as the house is being built.

Most owner-builders follow the pattern outlined above, but some take their design further before beginning construction and some do not go as far. The personality of the individual owner-builder and the nature of the project seem to determine the extent of the pre-construction design work. But, no matter how much effort is expended perfecting the design, it is always incomplete at the time construction begins. In every case, there are decisions that have been postponed.

Owner-builders postpone these decisions for very practical reasons. So many decisions must be made to draw a complete set of plans that owner-builders eventually find unavoidable the alternative of starting to build, taking the problems as they come. The sheer quantity of information needed to make intelligent decisions tends to overwhelm inexperienced owner-builders. They postpone decisions until the construction phase, because they feel they will have more opportunity to learn about something in which they are actively involved than about something they are planning. Owner-builders will easily learn more about plumbing, for example, when they are involved in the activities of buying materials, fitting the pieces together, and asking specific questions of a plumber friend, than when they are planning for these activities before construction has begun.

The manner in which materials are purchased gives owner-builders another reason for designing as they build. Since they can rarely afford (nor are they inclined) to buy all their materials before construction begins, owner-builders seldom know at that time exactly what materials they will be using. It is frequently the case, for example, that owner-builders will want to begin construction before they have acquired all their windows. It is therefore necessary to leave their plans somewhat open-ended, so that these undiscovered materials can be incorporated into the house.

Owner-builders should not be afraid to experiment. Alternative solutions may need to be tested before the desired proportions are found.

With the design-as-you-build process, owner-builders are able to consider things in relationship to one another, while actually looking at the things being considered. The placement of windows is a typical example of how this situation can work to their advantage. When they can see how the window will work in relationship to the site and to the rest of the building, that is the most opportune time to make the decisions of how to place the window—what shape and what size they want it to be. If an owl's nest is discovered atop a distant tree, a tiny window can be added to frame the view. If a view of a river is discovered to have a stronger effect than originally imagined, a window can be enlarged. The relationship of walls to one another, windows to walls, windows to the landscape, the way that light enters the room, the placement of electrical lighting—all of these things can be best understood by actually seeing them in place.

Since improvement is progress, owner-builders should not hesitate to dismantle and rebuild completed work. The change is most easily made at the time it is first discovered, and if it is made, the owner-builders will not have to live with any regrets.

Almost all owner-builders move into their houses long before they are "completed," despite well-founded warnings against this practice. If they are willing to put up with the inconveniences, they can take advantage of the situation. Since all the activities of daily living will be taking place in the spaces designed to accomodate them, owner-builders are in a good position to see how they might change the design to make it more functional. Better placement of a doorway, for example, is often discovered after the house has been occupied. By leaving out a section of wall, the newly discovered doorway can be accomodated. The adjustments and changes normally made to a house after it has been completed can now be made as the owner-builders finish the house in which they are living.

Living in the house while it is under construction can also adversely affect the design. The problem is that design decisions are often influenced by the temptation to take shortcuts in order to hasten the improvement of living conditions. Owner-builders will be tempted to choose the fastest solution whereas, had they not been living in the house, the best solution would hav been chosen. Substitutions are made—aluminum sliders for hand-crafted

This owner-built house is well built and well designed in every respect except that the large bank of south-facing windows makes the space unbearably hot in summer. This mistake was made because the inexperienced owner-builder designed his house in the winter.

French doors, indoor-outdoor carpeting for tile floors, porcelain tubs for wooden ones. These design decisions are usually regretted after the house has been "completed."

There are problems with the design-as-you-build method, even if the owner-builders do not move in early. The major problem is that the method involves a linear decision-making process. Each design decision made in the process of building causes unpredictable effects. This problem is more crucial when the designer is a novice. One owner-builder, for example, decided to put a huge window in the gable wall adjacent to his loft. Then, he realized that a vent pipe had to run through the same area. The decision about where to run the vent pipe, could it have been made independent of the first decision, would have been to run the vent through the same gable wall—clearly the best route. But now the presence of the window in the wall prevented the vent from passing; the first decision had stymied the second. Had this owner-builder been able to make the two decisions simultaneously, two smaller windows would probably have been used with the vent running between them. The owner-builder who called his house "the temple of accumulated error" was not merely talking through his hat.

Case History

Tenold and Karen's Converted Carport Complex

FIRST FLOOR

SECOND FLOOR

cost $3,500
sq. feet 760
cost/sq. ft $4.60

0   5   10   15   20 FT

Description

This little complex is built on pressure-treated poles. The ground floor of the main structure includes kitchen, dining, general work space, storage, and a sleeping nook (southwest corner). The large doors at the east end of this space open outside to a covered storage/work space, which doubles as a summer kitchen. A recycled fire escape at the west end of the main space leads through a trap door to the bedroom above. The bath house/laundry is a separate building, connected to the main building by means of a walkway and a stairway.

The ground floor of the main structure is a concrete slab. The stud walls, infilled between the poles, are sheathed with plywood covered with hand-split cedar shakes on the exterior and are sheetrocked on the interior. The bedroom is conventionally framed except for the poles in the north wall which are continuous from the first floor. The walls of both the bedroom and bath house are sheathed with cedar on the interior, and plywood with tarpaper on the exterior—awaiting their cedar shakes. All the walls are insulated with fiberglass batt insulation. The pitched roofs are insulated with 1" styrofoam and covered with corrugated metal roofing. The deck and walkways are roofed with 90 lb. rolled roofing. The doors were salvaged, but the windows, many of them stained glass, were made by Tenold.

The main space is heated by the wood cook stove, and the bedroom and bath house each have a wood heat stove. Water is pumped from a deep well and is heated in coils which pass through the kitchen and bath house stoves. Sewage from the bath house drains into a septic system, but the kitchen sink, which is downhill

from the septic tank, drains into a leach pit.

Comments

Tenold is a sculptor/stained glass artist who made a living teaching art

at a southern California college. He had just bought five acres in the country when he and Karen, also an artist, got together in the summer of 1972. Both Tenold and Karen had lived most of their lives in cities, and both were intrigued by the idea of moving to a rural setting and becoming more self-sufficient. But, since their livelihood was centered in the city, they were able to spend only the summer months in the country.

That first summer they camped out on the new property, building a bridge and a sleeping platform. The following summer they returned and obtained a building permit to build a carport. They wanted a dry place in which to store some belongings, because they felt they would soon be moving to the country permanently.

Although it wasn't planned that way, the carport turned out to be quite unique. Because the pole manufacturer ran out of short poles, five of the 16 roof supporting poles were extremely long. Shortening these long poles seemed wasteful, so Tenold and Karen decided to use them to support another smaller roof above the main roof. This would give

them more storage space, and they thought perhaps the little space could be used later as a greenhouse. At the end of the summer, when they returned to the city, they left a 16'x28' carport with a 12'x16' gazebo on its roof.

When they returned the following summer, Tenold and Karen had come to stay. They first enclosed the two-story carport to provide a warm, dry place for the winter. Then they built the bath house and had the septic system installed (it will serve a future house). They wired both the carport and bath house and started on the water system and interior finish.

About a year after they started, the place was sufficiently complete for them to move on to new projects. They are currently building a large studio/workshop (with a permit) where they plan to conduct summer workshops. Their future house eventually will be attached to this studio, and their present quarters, originally conceived as a carport, will become a guest house.

It is interesting that all construction (except electrical and

septic) has been done on the original carport permit which expired before most of the work had been started.

8. Construction

In the previous chapter, it was pointed out that owner-builders start building their houses before their plans have been finalized. In this chapter, we shall discover that, in most cases, owner-builders also begin their houses before they possess the skills they will need to build them.

Starting to build without either plans or construction skills makes owner-builders quite unique. People in "primitive" societies build houses without explicit plans, but they are familiar with the materials and the construction techniques they will use. Today's owner-builders, on the other hand, have little in the way of skills or knowledge to compensate for their lack of complete plans. Yet, many owner-builders manage to build houses that are both aesthetically and functionally successful. How are they able to do this?

Not everyone has the attitude and the physical ability necessary to begin a house and proceed to a successful conclusion. But most people, once they have made the initial decision to proceed, do find these qualities in themselves. Success is more a matter of determination than of previous experience. Initial hesitation and lack of confidence are common and understandable. Even the simplest of tasks are more difficult the first time they are attempted, and there are myriad tasks which must be learned in order to build a house. But, once prospective owner-builders overcome their initial hesitation, once they become confident of their ability to learn the necessary skills, their ultimate success becomes likely.

The success of inexperienced owner-builders is possible because, almost without exception, they choose a system of construc-

Mike and Sandy have spent three weeks of vacation plus every weekend for five months laying 90 tons of rock for the stem walls of their log garage/guest house. They plan to live in the guest house while taking five years to build their 2,750 sq. ft. log house.

tion that has been tried and proven. Whether it is a log cabin, a dome, an adobe, a post and beam, or a stud frame structure, owner-builders will be able to learn from the successes and failures of others. How-to-do-it literature for each of these systems is available and not hard to find.

It is not surprising that the greatest amount of literature pertains to the construction system used most frequently—the stud frame system. But, owner-builders using other systems can, and usually do, take advantage of the voluminous stud-frame literature, as well. The basic principles of foundations, stairways, fireplaces, electrical and plumbing systems, etc., are the same regardless of the system used to construct the shell of the house.

Probably even more important than how-to-do-it literature is the advice that can be gleaned from experienced people. Material suppliers have always been a good source of information for do-it-yourselfers. They are interested in selling a product and can usually tell their customer how to install that product. Even more useful than material suppliers, however, are the owner-builders' experienced friends and neighbors. These people, aside from being such a convenient source of information (often providing on-site advice), can provide insights obtainable from no other source. Unlike literature, these people can give advice based on local conditions. Unlike material suppliers, they have no ulterior motives to sell a particular method or material. With the recent surge in owner-builder activity, the number of experienced builders has increased rapidly. This has made more information available to owner-builders and will undoubtedly improve the quality of owner-built houses in the future.

Although house building is a process demanding a number of skills, it is essential for first-time owner-builders to recognize that these skills can be acquired during the course of construction in a fashion similar to the way in which the design itself develops—bit by bit, as the need arises. In this sense, the construction and design processes are inseparable. Both develop simultaneously, and each affects the other. As the merits of alternative roofing materials are weighed, for example, one of the factors to be examined will be the skills needed to install each alternative. When a roof is finally chosen and the time comes to install it—this is when the details of the installation procedure will be learned, because this is when they need to be learned.

The new tasks attempted by owner-builders can be learned with relative ease because they are based on methods and materials that have been developed to allow houses to be built quickly and easily. These methods have evolved because they are uncomplicated, easy to learn, and easy to implement. One of the most significant achievements in this direction occurred over 100 years ago when George Washington Snow invented the balloon frame system of building. This new system soon replaced the time-consuming hand-hewn post and girt system that had been in use until that time. It was proclaimed that, "A man and a boy can now (1865) attain the same results, with ease, that twenty men could on an old-fashioned frame."[1]

Since that time, there have been many developments that have made the construction of houses even easier. The framing system has been simplified further, power tools have been introduced and materials such as plywood and plastics have been developed. Recently invented pneumatic fastening systems have made it possible to build a house without having to swing a hammer.

Mexican Americans, working through Self-Help Enterprises, a government sponsored cooperative self-help housing program, have successfully built over 1,000 houses in southern California.

Plumbing and electrical systems, introduced to the house around 1900, have been simplified to the extent that almost no tools are needed to install them. Today, it is possible to plumb an entire house without using a pipe wrench. Plastic pipes can be cut with a hand saw before being glued together.

Skills are most easily acquired when the tasks involved can be repeated several times. Repetition is a natural way for owner-builders to learn, since building a house is essentially a series of repetitive tasks. Each task becomes easier with successive attempts until the operation is finally mastered. The owner-builder constructing a concrete block wall, for example, will have to learn to mix mortar and to set each block in the mortar so that it is in line, level, and plumb. Setting the first block will probably be quite difficult, but the experience will make setting the second block easier. After several blocks have been set, a level of competence will have been reached that will carry through to the completion of the wall. This mechanism of learning by repetition is encountered in almost every phase of house construction—building a stud wall, shingling, installing windows, plumbing, wiring, putting struts on a

Experimental owner-builders sometimes encounter tasks for which no tool exists. This man is patching his dome using a heat sealer fashioned from a light bulb, two lenses, an orange juice can, and a vacuum cleaner.

dome, etc. It is an important consideration for prospective owner-builders who lack confidence in their construction skills.

Owner-builders will sometimes test their abilities by constructing a practice building. This structure usually takes the form of a barn, storage shed, or workshop to be associated with the house as an out-building. (These are the buildings that are frequently occupied "temporarily" while the house is being built.) This practice is highly recommended, especially if the form of the out-building resembles the proposed form of the future house. By doing this, owner-builders can acquaint themselves with many of the procedures they will eventually use in the construction of the house. Difficulties will be encountered before the house is started and, in addition to developing their construction skills, the experience will help in planning the construction of the house.

It is important for owner-builders to realize that there is a single, most efficient procedure for constructing every house. This procedure involves the common sense layering of materials, one over the other, in a specific sequence. Contractors, who must pay for labor, are very aware of the importance of this principal and direct a great part of their efforts toward controlling the sequence of work on a building. The best sequence permits all workers to work continuously, without doing anything twice and without stumbling over other workers or over materials or equipment. Owner-builders are also concerned with minimizing the time and effort needed to build their houses, but there are influences which tend to direct them away from that ideal sequence requiring the least work. These influences include:

PSYCHOLOGICAL INFLUENCES. There is a tendency among owner-builders to first construct those parts of the house which have the most dramatic impact. There is a sense of accomplishment and excitement accompanying a pronouced change which is lacking in the more tedious and slow-moving tasks. It should be recognized that this can lead to extra work later on. More than one owner-builder has tired of shingling the roof, only later to spend many hours sanding water-stained ceilings.

INFLUENCE OF COLLECTING INFORMATION. It has been noted that owner-builders often delay construction in order to collect as much information as possible. The result of this practice is that construction phases requiring the most information (such as plumbing and wiring systems) are often postponed until the last possible moment. The difficulties can be minimized if owner-builders manage to divide these complicated systems into stages. If, for example, plumbing problems are at least briefly researched early in the construction process, owner-builders can later save themselves from such useless and aggravating projects as knocking a hole in a foundation wall through which to pass a drainage pipe.

INFLUENCE OF DESIGNING AS YOU BUILD. Since the design of their house is usually incomplete, owner-builders must avoid construction that will limit the possibilities for future design decisions. If the position of a window hasn't been decided, for example, it is logical to erect the wall which will contain that window without first sheathing it. The window can then be positioned in relation both to the outline of the wall and to the potential views. The task of sheathing the wall must be postponed in order to make this design decision possible, even though the wall could be sheathed much more easily before it is erected. The incompleteness of the design has the effect of delaying construc-

This temporary kitchen was set up on a living room wall so that the owner-builders could move in early. They cooked on a temporary wood cook stove and carried water for six months.

tion in order to keep alternatives open.

INFLUENCE OF MOVING IN EARLY. Most owner-builders move into their houses long before they have finished building them. Beside cluttering the house with objects which must be moved or worked around, early occupation has the effect of altering the sequence of construction. This happens because there is an urgency to complete those aspects of the house which most affect the functions of daily living. The importance of such things as running water, counter space, lighting, privacy, and heating increases greatly when the house is occupied. An understanding of the principles of sequence is critical here, since owner-builders are suddenly faced with the prospect of installing several of the most complicated systems of the house.

Prospective owner-builders should not let their inexperience discourage them from building a house, but they should realize that their project will consume much more time than they can possibly imagine. If determination is the most essential emotion for launching owner-built projects, then perseverence and patience must head the list for concluding these projects. Owner-builders will have to spend time discovering how to do things and there to get the materials to do them. They will make mistakes that will have to be corrected. They will be unaware of short cuts. They will use inadequate tools and will pay attention to detail where it is not needed. When making estimates of time, in fact, owner-builders should learn to be extremely conservative, lest they be consistently disappointed. As a rule of thumb, even conservative time estimates by inexperienced owner-builders can usually be doubled.

Despite the seemingly endless procession of interminable tasks, building a house is often described as one of the most fulfilling experiences of one's life. The gratification of learning so many new things, the satisfaction of creating with one's one hands, and the excitement of seeing the spaces evolve, help to compensate for the long hours of hard work. But, in the end, it is a vision of the finished product, the place where one can sit back and forget about all the work it takes to build that place, that makes it worthwhile.

Many owner-builders, when they see that a professional can build a house in six weeks, expect to be able to build their own house during a summer. For a variety of reasons, their expectations are seldom fulfilled. This owner-built house is in a typical state of completion as the end of the summer approaches—no plumbing, temporary electricity, and polyethylene film windows.

John and Abbie's House

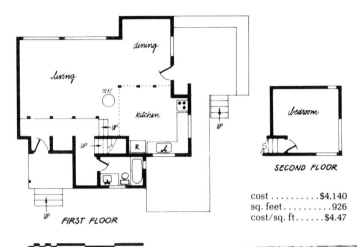

SECOND FLOOR

cost $4,140
sq. feet 926
cost/sq. ft $4.47

UP FIRST FLOOR

0   5   10   15   20 FT

Description

This frame house on six acres has three levels. The main level includes a kitchen, a dining area, a living area, and outside, a large east and south-facing deck. The entrance level, two feet above the main level, includes a front porch, entry halls, and a bathroom. The single bedroom above the kitchen is on the top level.

Since conventional construction details were used throughout, the house distinguishes itself from ordinary housing only in its spatial characteristics and by the inventive use of inexpensive materials. The house sits on a continuous block foundation and has 2x4 stud walls which support exposed-rafter ceilings. The walls are insulated with fiberglass batts, the ceilings with 1" rigid insulation. Windows and doors are all salvaged except the front door which was made from scratch. Water is pumped from a downhill spring and drains into a septic system. Heat comes from a pot-belly stove located in the center of the house. All work with the exception of the septic system and the sheetrock taping was done by the owners and their friends.

Comments

It was the beginning of the summer, 1970, when John and Abby decided it would be a good idea to build a house for themselves. John was an architecture student with two years of school remaining, and he liked the idea of getting practical experience in the discipline he was studying at

WEST ELEVATION

school. Even though he had considerable construction experience, he had never built anything to code and was particularly interested in learning about this. He was also interested in learning exactly how much it would cost to build an owner-built house. (Exact records were kept and are listed in Appendix B.)

Since they were particular about finding a secluded building site with a good supply of surface water, John and Abby spent the greater part of the summer looking for land. They finally found a site, and John hastily designed a house with the intent that it should be as small and simple as possible while taking full advantage of the unique setting. Plans were drawn, a permit was obtained, and construction was begun; but by the time school had started again in the fall, only the concrete footings had been completed.

John finished the foundation bit by bit during the school year. The

following summer Abby's brother, Bradford, arrived hoping to learn something about house construction. With his help, the outside of the house was finished and a 12'x24' workshop built by the end of the summer. At this point John and Abby moved into their unfinished house, storing most of their belongings in the workshop. They ran extension cords from the temporary power supply, cooked on a wood cook stove, carried water from a neighbor's house, bathed in a galvanized tub, and used an outhouse for about five months. John was attending school and installing the plumbing, electricity, and water supply systems in his spare time.

By the following autumn, two years after the footings were poured and one year after it was first occupied, the house was very near completion. John and Abby lived there for two more years before they sold the house and moved on to start all over again.

9. Economics

Owner-built housing can be less expensive than any other type of low-cost housing currently available in this country; i.e. tract housing, modular housing, and mobile homes. The reason is that owner-builders do not have to pay for labor, sellers' fees, or interest. They must only buy materials, substituting their own time for the money they would otherwise have had to pay other people.

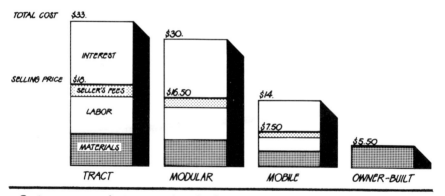

Cost per square foot comparing the least expensive of each type of low-cost housing with an owner-built house of comparable caliber. Interest is based on a 20 year loan at 7%. Relative figures are more important than absolute values which will change with time and location.

Despite the lower total cost, owner-builders frequently have difficulty paying for their house. This is because they must bear the entire cost of the house within a relatively short period of time. The tract house buyer and the mobile home buyer spend considerably more in the long run, but they pay in small installments spread over a long period of time—a small down payment followed by monthly

This three bedroom, two bathroom, 3,500 square foot house was built for $3.30 per sq. ft. in 1973.

payments usually lasting 20 to 30 years. Owner-builders, on the other hand, must accumulate the entire cost of their house before it can even be completed. Many prospective owner-builders are discouraged from building when they realize the magnitude of this initial financial burden.

Banks and government lending institutions could ease this burden by making loans available to owner-builders, but they are reluctant to do so. Banks lend money for the purchase of building materials only when assurances have been made that the house assembled from those materials can be easily sold on the open market. This requirement assures the bank that the loaned money could be recovered if the borrower should default. Unfortunately for owner-builders, the requirement conflicts with their approach to building. Their penchant for personalizing their house, their untested craftsmanship, and their tendency to leave things unfinished all weaken the argument that their house could be easily sold on the open market. Owner-builders simply do not fit the banks' definition of "a good risk."

The federal government, with its vast financial resources and its purported interest in boosting housing starts, is in the most logical position to assist owner-builders financially. A close approximation of real financial assistance once came through the Farmer's Home Administration, a former branch of the FHA, which loaned money to low-income rural owner-builders who could demonstrate proficiency in house construction. Current FHA regulations, however, require that a bonded contractor perform the construction. Why couldn't the government insure low-interest no-strings-attached owner-built housing loans in the same way it insures student loans? Most owner-built homes cost less than the $6,000 a student can borrow in four years, and they constitute tangible property which could be sold should the borrower default.

Since financial assistance is not available, owner-builders must work with their own, often limited funds. The realization of their project depends on their ability to keep the initial cost of construction as low as possible and/or their ability to spread the cost over a long period of time.

Of paramount importance in keeping construction costs low is the owner-builders' ability to locate and utilize inexpensive materials. In this pursuit, they have one great advantage over contractors. This advantage is time. Owner-builders have time to scrounge for materials, sometimes finding them at no cost. They have time to visit salvage yards and auctions for used materials—windows, fixtures, etc. They have time to shop around for new materials, picking up bargains when they appear, buying materials at their seasonal low price. The importance of time as a money-saving factor for owner-builders cannot be overstressed. Used materials not only take more time to obtain than new materials; they are also more time consuming to install. Free materials are available because much time is required to make them useful.

Owner-builders are elated when they find a source of free materials. Of most interest are those materials which can be used directly, with little or no alteration—materials such as lumber, windows, fixtures, pipes, wiring, and bricks. These materials, commonly found in old barns, houses, churches, and commercial buildings, are sometimes acquired merely for the asking. The owner will give them to anyone willing to demolish the building and haul the materials away. Rural fire departments in northern Washington have lists of farmers who want their old, unused farm

A family of five has lived in this 24 foot plydome for two years while trying to save enough money to build a more permanent house. The mother of the family says, "I'm tired of hearing how spiritual it is to live in a dome. People are always talking about the Indians. I'd really like to have electricity so I could have a vacuum cleaner."

92

This church is being dismantled in exchange for all salvageable materials. Owner-builders are frequently turned away from such sources of free material because of the liability risk. A legal liability disclaimer which can eliminate this risk is reprinted in Appendix A.

buildings burned for tax purposes. Owner-builders in that area have been fortunate to obtain the names of these farmers who may prefer to have their old buildings torn down and hauled away as to have them burned.

When purchasing materials for their house, it is to the owner-builders' great advantage that they are shopping for themselves. Unlike contractors, they need not be concerned with satisfying the prevailing public taste. Owner-builders are free to buy whatever pleases them, no matter how marred or strange it may appear to the next person. This freedom, although it seems quite obvious, should be not underestimated in its importance to owner-builders, since it allows them to buy used, damaged, discontinued, and low-grade materials that contractors cannot buy.

One of the easiest ways for owner-builders to minimize the initial cost of their house is to make the house as small as possible. The smaller the house, the fewer materials will be needed, and the less it will cost to build and heat. Owner-builders often take advantage of this relationship, designing their house to the minimum size that will accomodate their immediate needs. Almost every house in this book includes fewer than 1,000 square feet of floor area. If care is not taken, however, this effort to economize by minimizing the size of the house can easily result in a house that is too small. A large percentage of owner-builders feel that they initially designed their house too small.

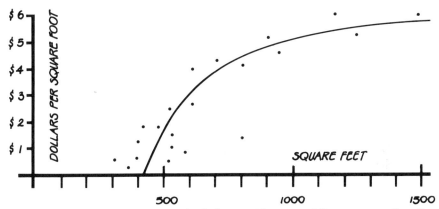

Each dot represents an owner-built house. The curved line representing the average of these instances shows the trend that owner-builders who spend less per square foot also tend to build smaller houses.

Of course, the cost of a house is not directly proportional to its size since the cost of water, power, and heating systems are chiefly related to the complexity of the system itself. By simplifying these systems, owner-builders can make substantial savings in the initial cost of construction. The cost of a wood stove, for example, is so much lower than the cost of conventional electric or forced air heating systems that over half of the owner-builders in this book chose wood heat as their primary heating source. But the decision to substitute a cheaper, simpler system for the traditional one is generally made at the expense of convenience. A latrine is certainly less expensive to build than a flush toilet with its accompanying septic system, but it is hardly as convenient on a cold rainy night.

Finding inexpensive materials, minimizing the size of the house, and simplifying the heating, the power, and the water systems all help owner-builders to keep the cost of their house at a minimum. But the financial burden can be eased even further if they are able

The living room of a house built by an artist who traded paintings for many of his materials.

to spread the cost over a long period of time, building their house bit by bit, completing things as they can afford them. This turns out to be a natural strategy for owner-builders since they usually take a long time to build their house regardless of their financial situation. The usual pattern (averaging about two-to-three years) is to build the shell of the house first, move in, complete the heating, power, and water systems as soon as possible, and leave the finish work until last. This lengthy construction period can easily be extended to accomodate a lack of funds. (One family lived in their unfinished house for six years before the flush toilet was installed.) Despite the inconvenience, this tactic is particularly important to owner-builders with limited funds, since it allows them to design their house around their long-range needs rather than around their immediate financial means.

A successful variation of this strategy is the practice of living in a hastily-erected out-building, while the more substantial house is being constructed. Several families cited as examples in this book (see pages 66, 74, 144) have adopted this approach and recommend it highly. Their temporarily outfitted studios, workshops, and barns provide relative comfort during the extended house construction period, and they eliminate the conflicts which arise from simultaneously living in and working on the same building.

Owner-builders are notorious for under-estimating the cost of their house. This is principally due to their inexperience at estimating the amount of materials needed. The finsihed house often costs 25-50% above the original estimate. We feel that owner-builders could approximate the true cost of their house with much more accuracy if they were able to gauge their own estimate from examples of other owner-built houses. In the interest of providing such an example, a complete cost breakdown of the house pictured on page 86 is included in Appendix B.

Scott takes pride in building economically. His house is built of lumber cut from windfallen trees with a portable mill. It is supported on concrete collected free from concrete trucks returning with partial loads, and is weatherproofed with recycled aluminum photo-offset plates.

Ron and Janet's A-Frame

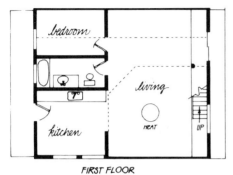

FIRST FLOOR

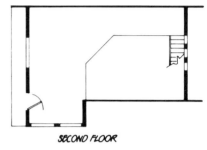

SECOND FLOOR

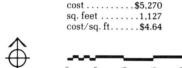

cost $5,270
sq. feet 1,127
cost/sq. ft. $4.64

0   5   10   15   20 FT

Description

This A-frame on a two-acre lot has a loft and a two-story dormer. The first floor contains a living area, a kitchen, a bathroom, and a small bedroom. There is a narrow porch at either end. The second story loft is open to the first floor. The house appears much larger in plan than it actually is since the walls slope-in considerably. (A six foot person will bump his head on the wall when his feet are three feet from its base.)

The 4x10 A's are bolted five feet on center to a continuous concrete foundation. Economy grade 2x8 tongue and groove decking is nailed to the outside of these A's to form the exposed wall/ceiling. The decking is covered on the outside with 1" styrofoam insulation which in turn is covered with cedar shakes. The gable walls are stud construction sheathed inside and out with cedar boards and insulated with fiberglass batts. Water comes from a well and drains into a septic system. Heat comes from a circular stone fireplace with a metal hood and from a small wood heater in the loft. All materials for the building were purchased new except for the windows.

Comments

Ron and Janet first started thinking about building their own house when they decided it was foolish to pay $1,500 a year for rent. That money, they figured, could be applied toward a house of their own. Even though they didn't have any money, they started designing their house. When relatives offered to loan them money to build, they accepted gratefully.

They bought land and a teepee and moved to the site. The house they

EAST ELEVATION

wanted to build was an A-frame. Ron had always been fascinated by A-frames. He liked the high ceilings and the opportunity to include lofts easily. He figured it would be easy to build because of the simple structural system and the fact that the ceiling and walls are one and the same. Simplicity of design and of construction were of particular importance to Ron since he had never designed or built anything except a pair of speaker cabinets.

The design was drawn with a straightedge on graph paper only to meet the requirements for a building permit. Ron claims that the ideas for the building were so firm in his mind that drawings were not necessary for his own enlightenment. He even refused to consult books during the time the house was being designed. He wanted the design to be entirely his own idea, without any outside influences. "I've always had strong ideas about how I wanted my own house to be," he said. "When I finally got the chance to build it, I wasn't about to stand aside and listen to someone else tell me how it should be done."

Construction began in late spring, and by mid-summer the basic shell had been completed. The building was about five feet shorter than originally planned since the position of some trees had prevented the

erection of the last "A," and since Ron had mistakenly cut the overhang too short. The shortness of the building necessitated a reorganization of the interior spaces. The kitchen and bathroom were reduced in size to make room for a bedroom—moved downstairs because a loft at the east end of the building had to be eliminated. The entire structure, to this point, had been constructed without the aid of a plumb, a level, or a square.

At this stage, with the shell complete, Ron and Janet decided to move out of their teepee into their new house. The house was far from complete—no water, no power, no windows or doors, and no shakes on the roof—but the tempatation proved too much to resist. They lived in and worked on the house for over a year before deciding that an A-frame wasn't really the kind of house they wanted. They bought a lot across the street where they are presently building another house.

Section Three

The Owner-Builder and The Code

This section documents the conflicts between owner-builders and the codes. We suggest how these conflicts might be minimized through evasive techniques or through revision of the codes.

10. The Western Scene

It is not by accident that the United States, the standard-bearer of consumptive societies, has produced a strain of people who reject the notion of mindless acquisition. In the midst of proliferating technology, there are those who favor simpler, more humane means toward "progress." As the masses, directly or indirectly, condone the pillaging of nature's resources, a growing minority learns to conduct itself sensitively toward the delicate eco-systems. And in a culture of specialization, where services are contracted for a price and where necessities are sold by huge corporations, people can be found learning through their own initiative to provide for themselves. Do-it-yourself information has always been available, but the social revolution of the Sixties has transformed self-sufficiency from hobby to way-of-life. Do-it-yourselfism has been elevated from fix-it projects around the house to the actual construction of the house.

Logically, much of the energy for self-sufficiency has been directed toward the country, where land availability has provided the arena for hand-skill learning and experimentation. Urban expatriates, the backbone of the back-to-the-land movement, theorized that the rural setting would be devoid of the panoply of laws and ordinances which strictly govern the cities. This has proven to be a misconception for many owner-builders and will be examined in this chapter.

Owner-builders cannot be categorized as a particular social group—basically they are inner-directed people who pick up a hammer for themselves when necessity calls. In the country, people have always followed such impulses and have often stood in singular defiance of state-mandated codes which impinge upon their freedom to "do it their own way," free of government sanction or prohibition.

This chapter will focus on the large numbers of people who have migrated from the cities, bought land, and attempted to have a direct hand in the shaping of their environment. Attention will be paid to their interaction with code-enforcing agencies and to how the codes have been used to deter their enthusiasm and endeavors.

Around 1968, with the demise of "flower power" and with the Vietnam War droning along endlessly, large numbers of people came to the realization that urban politics were inextricably mired. Paying high rents to absentee landlords, drawing gas and electricity from power companies, buying food from Safeway, watching aesthetically-pleasing old buildings being replaced by faceless high-rises, pavement continually being poured, and cars and people increasing in numbers under smoggy skies—these were realities which struck much closer to home than the bombing of North Vietnam, although affecting changes in either situation seemed equally futile.

In California, many began seeking their Mecca in the population-sparse counties to the north and east of San Francisco, hopeful that here they would have more opportunity to shape their environment and improve the quality of their lives. California, however, was by no means the only state to experience an urban-to-rural migration—it occurred in virtually all of the United States. Journals and magazines appeared, popularizing the movement and providing back-to-the-land information. Land was sold by thousands of acres to these primarily young self-styled pioneers from middle-class backgrounds. The vision for many was a form of neo-homesteading—buy land, build homes, raise animals, grow food; in short, become self-sufficient. When the war economy failed, they hoped not to be tied to it.

Of course, their inexperience was accompanied by a measure of naivete—shuyster realtors capitalized on the homesteaders' enthusiasm by making false promises and selling them land deemed useless by locals at grossly inflated prices. Means of financial support were unclear to most, although their arts and crafts industry and a resilient faith would, hopefully, see them through.

The land-reclamation revolution was replete with spiritual as well as political and social expectations. In the city, a source of alienation, if not spiritual imbalance, had been the disconnection between people and the fundamental energy sources which power their lives—food, water, and warmth. There is disconcerting artificiality in a society which creates the illusion that food "grows" in supermarket produce sections and not of the earth. Or that water comes from faucets and heat from a thermostat.

Becoming one with nature by developing one's own life-support systems was a by-product of the group's spiritual eclecticism. Many people drew upon Eastern concepts of unity with life's processes for harmonious and integrated well-being. Of course, the prospect of building one's own shelter excited many, even those with urban rearing whose education never included manual skills. The educational level of the new "landed immigrants" was actually quite high, although their degrees were often viewed as tickets to white-collar slavery, empty institutional jobs, or as an end to student draft deferments.

With this sketchy, sociological perview as a backdrop, a look at some land-mark events between the neo-homesteaders and local authorities might shed some light on an ominous trend in code enforcement.

In the late 1960s, near the Berkeley hotbed of student activism, a community emerged in a place called Canyon. While a new lifestyle was being articulated on the San Francisco Bay Area campuses, it was being practiced in Canyon. Community consciousness ran high and resourcefulness was the mode, as people bought land and built houses amidst one of the world's furthest inland stands of redwood trees.

Canyon is a 125-year-old community of enduring beauty. Unlike their predecessors, Canyon's new residents treated their environment with reverence, considering beauty a resource in itself, not to be exploited. Betwen 1850 and 1860, with the advent of steam-powered saws, logging concerns had decimated Canyon's entire stand of first growth redwoods, destroying a natural point of reference for navigators steering their boats into San Francisco Bay. Canyon in time regained its natural splendor, thanks to the redwood's amazing regenerative powers (one stump can nurture the growth of up to 500 new trees.).

One of Canyons's environmental protectors, the East Bay Municipal Utilities District (EBMUD), ironically became a political enemy of the community's residents. EBMUD owned most of the property surrounding Canyon as park and watershed lands. Fearing that new development in Canyon would pollute the creek feeding one of its reservoirs, EBMUD in 1951 adopted a policy of vigorously pursuing the purchase of any Canyon property for sale. Each time land was secured by EBMUD, houses on the property were bulldozed. The community's population got smaller and smaller. EBMUD was also instrumental in influencing the county to proclaim a moratorium on building in Canyon. In the words of EBMUD's secretary:

> Any watershed that has septic tanks on it...is a hazard. This is working procedure in any water agency. Any waterman with a creek with septic tanks above it would be a fool if he didn't worry about it. [1]

Despite EBMUD's acquisitiveness, many people managed to buy existing houses and property in Canyon. When new property came up for sale, they organized collectively to out-bid EBMUD on the purchase. Disregarding the building moratorium, new houses of inventive design were constructed with whatever materials could be acquired.

Edifices of community integrity, such as the town's general store and post office, were reconstructed (without benefit of a permit) in a concerted volunteer effort by Canyon's many young, skilled carpenters. County authorities, in fact, were stunned by the refurbishing of the buildings and granted permits *post facto* to their reconstruction.

While some University of California's architecture students were encouraged to witness Canyon's innovative building techniques, county and EBMUD authorities were miffed by the community's self-assertiveness and solidarity of purpose. In February, 1969, a mysterious complaint to the county prompted a task force of 10 sheriff deputies, two state narcotics officers, a dog catcher, and three building inspectors to tag 16 illicit houses in Canyon. The "Do Not Enter" notices gave the residents 48 hours to remove the buildings, under the threat of a $500 fine or six months in jail.

If community recalcitrance was already known, the people's organizational skills and political savvy came to be known. Appealing to county officials on their own behalf, Canyon citizens hired lawyers and entered into lengthy litigation. They presented a proposal by a resident water resources expert, calling for a Canyon Special Services District. Everything about the district was to be contained within the community structure itself, from sewage to financing and operation. Waste water was to be treated and recycled within Canyon so that none could possibly pollute EBMUD's water supply. Also, with the waste removal problem solved, perhaps the county would again legitimatize building in Canyon.

The county rebuffed Canyon's proposals with opposing testimony coming from health department and EBMUD authorities. The plan was too innovative—a precedent for such a system did not exits. The taggings continued in April, 1969, as the houses were again posted for abatement as a public nuisance.

Lengthy abatement hearings began, during which Canyon people pleaded their case for permission to live and to build as they chose. Canyon residents retained consumer advocate and former Public Utilities Commissioner, William Bennett, as their spokesman. Bennett proclaimed:

> There is valid human reason to make allowances for the homes built by individuals in Canyon, just as individual allowances are made for older homes under 'grandfather clauses,' which exempt them from subsequent building codes.[2]

The Canyon story resolved happily for the owner-builders when the county officials, tired with the drawn-out battle and the unfavorable publicity, consented to a compromise. Or, perhaps they were embarrassed by the Canyon argument that temporary non-code housing for farm laborers was permitted within the county. Meanwhile, EBMUD abandoned its aggressive land policy and, in a new conciliatory climate, EBMUD bulldozers assisted Canyon locals in clearing a refuse dump site.

The compromise contained a promise from about one-half of the cited home-owners that they would move from their homes if given time to re-settle. Other home owners were given temporary septic tank permits, pending construction of new houses. Two other structures were reconsidered and labeled as "rooms" for existing houses. Future mass condemnations were to be eschewed by the county—hereafter, postings would be done on an individual basis. The septic tank requirements were amended so as not to be retroactive, and new houses could apply for permits.

Canyon, in turn, allowed itself to become a restricted community. No longer would it be a haven for squatters, transients, and campers. Reconciliation brought about a return to reason and the sanctification of a novel, creative community.

Perhaps the real reason for invoking the building codes in Canyon was that the ideas of the locals ran contrary to the intent of the area's big business interests. Resistance in Canyon to EBMUD's expansionism put it in the spotlight and with notoriety came the exposure which left it open to an official crackdown.

Building departments respond to complaints which many times have nothing to do with the question of health and safety. The departments, like all enforcement agencies, operate in a political-social atmosphere which, in part, predicates where authority is to be used. People who have access to the lines of communication with local authorities usually are those whose complaints com-

106

mand action.

Owner-building is an aspect of a wave of new consciousness toward life and its intrinsic values. In the social lag between the advent of new modes of thinking and lifestyles and between the ultimate assimilation of those ideas, the code is sometimes used as a bludgeon against those "guilty" of innovation. Where owner-building is characteristic of a new trend within a community, the codes can be a device used to terminate that activity. In this manner, they become instruments used to preserve the status quo and to stifle the evolution of new ways.

One of the first instances of a county using its ultimate power, demolition, against non-code housing occurred in the case of Lou Gottlieb and Morningstar Ranch. In 1966, Gottlieb, a visionary spiritualist and former folk singer with The Limeliters, had declared his Sonoma County, CA, acreage "open land." This encouraged a large influx from the cities of people who shared his vision of a cooperative community, dedicated to the preservation of Mother Earth.

The Morningstar experiment was enthusiastically received by

Lou Gottlieb, former Limeliter and founder of Morningstar Ranch, prior to the county demolition of 24 homes on his property.

hundreds of people. By June of 1967, there were 90 regulars at the ranch, with hundreds coming and going during the summer months. Twenty-four houses, ranging from shanty shacks of marginal material to more polished wood-framed endeavors, were constructed in rapid succession.

Morningstar Ranch soon suffered from overpopulation and, whenever the population increases, so does the social problem of human waste disposal. Notoriety within the larger Sonoma community led to an inspection of the premises by county building and health authorities. A court injunction against Morningstar followed. Gottlieb was ordered to clear the land of people, while facing a $500-a-day fine if the order was defied.

In Gottlieb's religious framework, human ownership of the earth was pretentious if not blasphemous. Refusing to evict people from a portion of nature deemed his by laws of property, Gottlieb was found guilty of contempt of court. Garnished from his bank account was a good portion of his savings ($14,000). In 1969, Sonoma County bulldozed all homes at Morningstar Ranch; except one, Gottlieb's, thus reinforcing the cultural assumption that all land has a responsible owner who lives in a private house.

Later that year, Gottlieb deeded his land to God. A famous case followed in which the same judge, who had ordered the bulldozing, ruled that God could not own land. In the words of the court:

> Whatever the nature of the Deity, God is not a person, natural or artificial, in existence at the time of conveyance and capable of taking title.

Besides evoking a curious judicial decision on the nature of God, the experience of Lou Gottlieb and Morningstar Ranch was interesting from the standpoint of code enforcement. A county had eliminated an experimental community by relieving its people of their homes.

To the north of Morningstar Ranch, a friend of Gottlieb's, Bill Wheeler, opened his 315 acres in Sonoma County, CA, to seekers of a spiritually-based co-operative community. The land was deeded to Ahimsa Church, as the community came to be known. Similar to Morningstar, Wheeler's Ranch emphasized unity with nature, freedom with responsibility, co-operation in place of competition, and group ownership instead of private property.

108

Bill Wheeler and Gay Leslie,
Wheeler's Ranch, 1972.

Wheeler's Ranch attracted literally thousands of people, although the regulars numbered the low hundreds. Problems developed over the access road which was designed for Wheeler's use but, to the chagrin of the neighboring rancher, was accomodating scores of "strange" people. While Bill Wheeler was being sued for removal of his access rights, a complaint lodged against nude swimming led to an inspection by a team of county health and building authorities.

In 1967, Bill had constructed a 24'x36' building of hand-hewn structural members with a continuous concrete foundation. He had an agricultural building permit to do so. Wheeler, an artist, intended to use the structure as a studio. The three-day inspection by county officials in May, 1969, resulted in the red-tagging of the studio and all other houses in the budding community. In the summer of 1969, a temporary injunction ordered people to leave the land. Sonoma officialdom, seeking to prevent "another Morningstar," declared Wheeler's Ranch a public nuisance and cited it for numerous building and health code violations. Ironically, and in the best spirit of back-to-the-land resourcefulness, wood from the moribund Morningstar had been recycled into the homes at Wheeler's.

Wheeler was prepared to go all the way to the Supreme Court in defense of his studio. A well-known law firm from San Francisco gave freely of its services on his behalf. His Constitutional attack on the building code was based on the fact that it was his land, his studio was built for himself, he had no intention to resell, etc.

The case fizzled when Wheeler, feeling a need for more humble quarters, vacated the studio and moved into a tent "to be closer to the land." His lawyer was dismayed, because the defense was built around a man's right to a shelter of his own creation. The judge nearly ordered him back into the studio.

In 1973, Sonoma County bulldozed 20 houses on Wheeler's Ranch. The people burned down 54 others to spare themselves the expense of having the county do it. Once again, people had been "protected" from their own choices.

The Wheeler-Ahimsa Church case eventually went to the Appellate Court, where the decision was upheld that conditions on the ranch endangered health and safety. Specifically, the court pointed to "lack of electrical lighting, lack of a required sewage disposal system, lack of an approved water supply, lack of proper water closets, lack of or improper kitchen sink, lack of hot and cold running water, improper heating facilties, etc."

Most of the charges are at least philosophically contestable—-can one not live healthfully without the amenities? In typical statutory double-think, "proper" and "approved" methods are only those given explicit mention in the law; alternatives are not for people to decide. Particularly galling must be the higher court finding that the ranch condition caused an "actual and impending threat to the enjoyment of life and property." To the ranch residents, life *was* enjoyable, at least prior to the county's intei.ention.

Bill Wheeler, a man who accomodates himself to change, reflects back on the history without rancor. He says, "What we had in the Ahimsa Church was a beautiful thing—we turned no one away, everybody got their share of love. Thousands of people came and went and, you know, to this day the only scars the land shows are the tracks of the county's caterpillars!"

A unique confrontation with building codes, without social overtones of "hippies" versus "straights," occurred in Eugene, Oregon, in 1975. This was Monte Marshall's individual resistance to the codes on grounds that they posed prior constriant on his art (architecture). In the classical stance of civil disobedience, Monte openly built and occupied a structure of non-code design, without permit, and challenged the city to prosecute him so that a Constitutional test of the codes could be made.

Monte Marshall's tetrahedrons, 1975.

Although Monte was a graduate of the University of Oregon's School of Architecture, his repugnance for building codes prevented him from seeking the license needed to practice as an architect. Two terms at the university's law school and an acute social sensitivity enabled Marshall to define his attack on the codes.

In 1972, Monte applied his study of structural theory by constructing two tetrahedrons on his lot within Eugene city limits. He received experimental permits from the city building department. The deviant design was permitted because the tetrahedrons were "statically indeterminant," which means their strength could not be calculated. Stress testing was to follow construction.

Despite the building department's flexibility, Monte's attitude toward the codes began to crystallize. He saw the building codes as interfering with his desire to create a system of low-cost housing, as contributing to the high cost of living, and unconstitutionally impinging upon the right of a human being to seek shelter. The system of submission of plans, specifications, and calculations for permits he saw as a prior constraint on his artistic freedom.

In precipitating his test case on the codes, Monte constructed a 35-foot-tall tetrahedron near the other two, while willfully ignoring the permit requirements of the building code. He recognized the responsibilities of the building officials and urged that they perform the procedural tasks of code enforcement against him.

He was charged with two misdemeanors, one for building without a permit, the other for illegal occupancy of an incomplete structure. He was found guilty, the permit charge being stayed indefinitely, while the city filed against him to force compliance with the occupancy regulations. The judge's decree ignored the Constitutional questions raised, leaving the decision for the federal judiciary.

Monte's central contention was that the code requirement for submission of designs prior to construction is analogous to a writer having to submit to a censorship board before publication. (Imagine us having to get a permit for this book!) He prided himself as being a foremost authority on a revolutionary design, the tetrahedron, and felt that he should be allowed to pursue his art without undue interference by government. In this regard, Monte's legal brief to the Circuit Court stated that he feels "works of art are incapable of being judged by conventional building code standards."

Monte's general ojections to the code are shared by many owner-builders:

> The Ninth Amendment reserves for the people certain intrinsic rights. I would argue that the right to shelter is a fundamental right. No matter how wise or sophisticated we think we are, we are all under an immediate compulsion to protect ourselves from the elements. We have to shelter ourselves. It's really synonomous with the right to life.
>
> No right is absolute. But what I do believe is that, in the final analysis, I have the right to build a non-standard or substandard dwelling, and the only constraint on that should be positive

proof that I have not endangered others.

But I also mean that if all you can afford is a tarpaper shack
to shelter yourself and your family, it's your right to build it—so
long as you don't endanger anyone else in the community. And I
mean really endanger, not just bringing someone's property
value down because you don't choose to live like them.[3]

Monte Marshall learned that attempting to move the courts to a
decision of wisdom is akin to Don Quixote attacking a windmill. The
Circuit Court judge ruled that he must vacate his tetrahedron
within 10 days or call the county jail his home for six months.
Sadly, he was no longer able to finance a federal court action on
the Constitutional issues. At the time of this writing, Monte
Marshall is attempting to comply with the court order.

The cases cited in this chapter demonstrate that code enforcement often transcends the issue of "the politics of building your
home." It becomes, for many, the politics of *losing* your home. Some
building inspectors behave as inquisitorial policemen, and the
courts act as janitors of social maintenance.

The stories of Canyon, Morningstar, and Wheeler's Ranch
established a precedent for the removal of a "public nuisance," in
these cases a euphemism for "social problem." A precedent was
set for accomplishing the delicate maintenance of social order by
bulldozing the homes of the "troublemakers." No homes, no
troublemakers.

Admittedly, the communards of the two ranches violated many
social customs of their more provincial neighbors. But, nude
sunbathing and trespassing are jobs for the sheriff, not the
building department.

The bulldozing examples led Mendocino County, Sonoma
County's northern neighbor, into an embarrassing situation, which
exposed "political code enforcement" (so-called by one ICBO
official) for what it is. It also brought attention to the failure of
"uniformity" and standardization in a dynamic world. And, most
importantly, it gave rise to the creation of United Stand, whose
articulation of the code's deficiencies has moved the California
state government toward an owner-builder amendment to the UBC.

Monte's Tetrahedrons

cost $5,000
sq. feet 1,860
cost/sq. ft $2.69

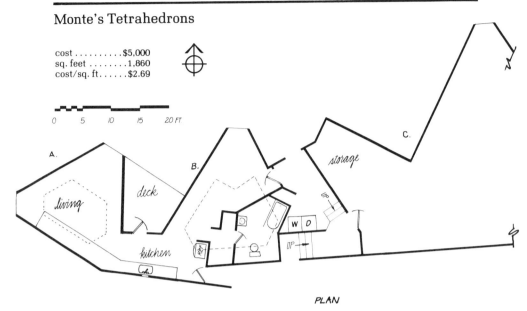

0   5   10   15   20 FT

A.

living

deck

kitchen

B.

W   D

UP

UP

storage

C.

PLAN

Description

There are three exploded tetrahedrons on a half-acre site in the city of Eugene, Oregon. The three are connected by means of conventional stud structures with flat roofs. The

two smaller tetrahedrons are completed to the point that they provide a functional living environment, and they are currently occupied by the owner and his family. The largest tetrahedron is planned to become the house eventually, but at this point, it is only a shell. The smaller two eventually will serve as a guest house and/or studio.

The basic structure of all three tetrahedrons consists of 2x4 lattices covered with ½" plywood. The lattices are stacked to make the equilateral triangles which form the faces of the tetrahedrons. The faces are covered with 1½" styrofoam insulation, 90 lb. rolled roofing, 1x4 stripping, and cedar shingles. The floor framing of the two smaller structures consists of double 2x4 joists framed triangularly and supported by posts on pier blocks. This framework is covered with ½" plywood and a particle board underlayment. The floor of the large tetrahedron is a concrete slab.

The entire complex was pneumatically stapled together. Seconds, rejects, blows, and shorts

were used for economy whenever possible. Water and sewer are connected to city systems. The two small tetrahedrons are heated electrically, but a tetrahedronal fireplace is planned for the large one.

Comments

Monte is a tetrahedron freak. He is building a three-tetrahedron house heated with a tetrahedronal fireplace. Behind the house are a tetrahedronal greenhouse and a tetrahedronal chicken coop.

Monte was employed as a drafting instructor at a community college when he decided to build his own house. A degree in architecture had prepared him well for designing a house, and his position as an instructor gave him the opportunity to test his ideas with his students. He soon finalized a concept for a 42 foot tetrahedron and, with the help of

some enthusiastic students, built the panels he would later assemble with a crane. Instead of erecting this monster, however, Monte decided to test his ideas with a smaller 18 foot tetrahedron. His plan was to build this smaller structure (A) so that he, his wife and son could live in it while constructing the large tetrahedron ultimately to be the house.

Only the framing of this small building was planned before construction began. Monte wanted to leave all other decisions to his intuition. He wanted the site and cost of materials to influence the design of the building as it was being built. When the framework was up, he decided the building was too small, and another small tetrahedron (B) was begun. The two tetrahedrons (A and B) were linked, plumbing and wiring was installed, and Monte and his family moved in. The house was small and unfinished, but they enjoyed all the basic conveniences except a shower or bath. No sooner had they moved in than Monte started work on the partially pre-assembled giant tetrahedron.

Seven months after the first tetrahedron (A) had been started, the giant tetrahedron had been erected but stood as a shell used only for storage. Monte was forced to stop working on it in order to install a bath in the smaller tetrahedrons occupied by his family. A bath is required by the city in order to obtain a

SOUTH ELEVATION

Certificate of Occupancy, and the city building department was threatening to shut off all utilities unless Monte complied with this regulation. He installed the bath, but he refused to apply for either a building permit or a certificate of occupancy. He continued building his tetrahedrons in defiance of all building codes.

In addition to philosophical arguments, Monte gave practical reasons for ignoring the codes altogether. He figured that, by taking this approach, he didn't have to worry about building his structures in contempt of any regulations since he had not agreed to follow any regulations in the first place. Had he obtained a permit, the building department would have demanded that he build the structures to code from the outset. By forging ahead without a permit, the building department would be put in the difficult position of having to make him demolish his completed structures and re-build them to code.

When, after more than two years of battling the city, Monte was faced with the choice of applying for a building permit or spending six months in jail, he finally acquiesced. He didn't have the money to carry his dispute to a higher court, and he had completed the largest percentage of his building anyway. He will have to finish his complex under the scrutiny of city building officials, but he will be working with satisfaction that, in the course of following his conscience, he had awakened the community to the conflicts between owner-builders and the building code.

11. United Stand

The story of United Stand graphically illustrates the extemes in code enforcement and how the codes are sometimes used to raze low-cost homes instead of promote them. It exposes the contradictions between code uniformity and individual self-determination. It also tells the story of an alliance of owner-builders who have successfully utilized the political process in defense of their homes.

The success and failure of United Stand is closely related to the legitimacy of the lifestyle which spawned the current wave of owner-building, and to the ability of democracy to permit that way of life. United Stand's strength is derived from the awareness that the right to shelter is inalienable. Its weakness is that universal infirmity—namely, perfunctory and selective treatment by disinterested government agencies.

The story of United Stand is a lesson in the art of affirmative political action, of common citizens uniting to implement their group will. The authors hope our readers will learn from the experience of United Stand. We hope this book will foster a political consciousness which will enable owner-builders to resist the tyranny of prohibitive government control over the act of people providing their own shelter.

Mendocino County, California, is located 80 miles north of San Francisco, in the central-to-northern portion of the state. Its coastline is unsurpassed in its beauty. Foggy coastal and river forests have produced magnificent stands of California Redwoods. Its flat to gently-rolling farm lands, wet winters, and dry, hot summers make Mendocino a leading producer of fine wines.

Gerry Herbert, one of over 100 Mendocino County owner-builders ordered to vacate and demolish their homes in the middle of winter.

Vineyards and trees, along with tourism, are the county's greatest resources. Yet, despite the success of these industries, Mendocino's general economy is depressed.

Land not owned by timber, wine, or ranch interests is often owned by affluent city people maintaining country homes. Many San Francisco-oriented artists live communally in this inspirational environment. The back-to-the-land movement discovered Mendocino naturally enough. Young people, seeking relief from the oppressive environment of the cities, began to purchase logged-over and low-utility parcels of land in the hills.

The people "took to the hills' and began developing homesteads. The conservative native residents viewed the newcomers skeptically. In some circles the dress, appearance, behavior, and general lifestyle of the newcomers was treated with hostility. A sentiment developed which stereotyped the new land-owners as freeloaders on welfare, non-contributors to the tax pool, and responsible for lowering neighboring land values.

The effect of the hill-folk in civic functions was not always well-received. They often required a more creative atmosphere for their children than that offered in the rural schools. Their presence required extended bus service and other "inconveniences" for the school district. It is said that people on the school board complained to county officials about the newcomers. Nude swimming and sunbathing were becoming commonplace, and complaints were filed about that, too. The young people in the hills found their public lives under scrutiny by the established locals, but as yet their private lives remained free from attack.

A short distance from Ukiah, the county seat, is an agricultural area known as Potter Valley. Mid-Mountain ranch is located in the hills above the valley. The ranch had been subdivided and sold to young people who were willing to hike in when their roads washed out, and who were resourceful enough to contend with the summer water shortage.

This home, built by United Stand defendants Brian and Pam Sorrells, was built with materials slavaged from a torn-down Grange hall.

In January, 1974, an airplane made continual passes over Mid-Mountain ranch, flying low enough for residents to see the pilot (despite minimum FAA ceiling regulations of 500 feet.) The plane hovered over the homesteads allowing the residents to draw the correct assumption that they were under surveillance. On February 5, 1974, a task force of building and health inspectors, a deputy sheriff, and a district attorney's representative ascended Mid-Mountain Road in four-wheel-drive vehicles. The task force put notices on several homes whose owners were away, declaring the premises "unfit for human occupance." Compliance with these notices meant the homes had to be vacated. Needless to say, when they returned home, unsuspecting occupants were shocked and terrified.

The scenario appeared to be Wheeler's Ranch Revisited. But one fundamental difference existed: the people given notice on Mid-Mountain were not members of a commune, openly challenging accepted cultural patterns. They were individual land-owners and tax-payers, quietly affirming the basic tradition of pioneer home-steading. Mendocino's task force carried one step further the police power exhibited in the Morningstar and Wheeler cases— *individual* property owners could now receive categorical treatment by authorities. The task force gave its own rendition of the nocturnal knock-on-the-door tactics Americans believe to exist in Communist countries. Due Process was ignored by the task force which made no prior announcement that an inspection was pending. The homeowners were not informed of the appeals process. They were simply told to leave and demolish their homes.

The Mid-Mountain community immediately made contact with a

NOTICE

PROHIBITED OCCUPANCY

THIS BUILDING IS UNFIT FOR HUMAN OCCUPANCY AND SHALL NOT BE OCCUPIED UNTIL APPROVED BY THIS DEPARTMENT AS COMPLYING WITH STATE LAW.

PROJECT ID Z-73-222-19
LOCATION Mid Mt Rd
DATE 2 May 1974

COUNTY of MENDOCINO
DEPARTMENT OF BUILDING INSPECTION
Lake Mendocino Drive
UKIAH, CALIFORNIA
Phone: 462-1408

DO NOT REMOVE THIS CARD

BUILDING INSPECTOR

The county's rationale was that a building needs a permit to exist—if it doesn't have a permit, it doesn't exist; therefore it cannot be brought up to code.

Ukiah lawyer. He assured them that the codes were negotiable, and that the inspectors were flexible. Ten days later, the same lawyer was told by county inspectors that the houses could not be brought up to code and that demolition was the only recourse.

Letters arrived shortly after the task force appearance. The letters informed the people that their structures were in violation of Mendocino County building, zoning and health codes. They were ordered to vacate and demolish their homes in 30 days or face formal action. The letters were signed by Chief Building Inspector, Donald Uhr, who was to emerge as the most intractable and biased of the county personnel. (One couple who hadn't even been tagged received an Uhr letter.)

Mendocino County Chief Building Inspector Donald Uhr warned against an invasion of "hippies and freaks" if the building code standards were lowered. Later he was to say that lifestyle was not the issue.

Another similarity can be drawn between the Mendocino taggings and the Canyon, Morningstar and Wheeler antecedents. The principals in each case were ordered to vacate and demolish their homes in mid-winter. Even California is wet and cold in the winter and, the code requirements notwithstanding, there were families living in the homes. To move their belongings down intraversable roads during the rainy season would be difficult to say the least.

The Mid-Mountain community was experienced in co-operative effort. Most of the land parcels were owned and developed by individual families, but the community jointly owned 20 acres on which a milling operation and an auto shop had been built. The taggings turned the people's energies away from homesteading and community development. Survival required that they organize against the destruction of their homes, which meant becoming political. An apartment was rented in Ukiah—eventually to serve as United Stand headquarters—where the people researched the codes, made important contacts, and sought solutions.

As the newly formed group began to gather information, it became obvious that task force enforcement was discriminant. The group discovered a prejudicial Grand Jury recommendation which had precipitated the creation of the task force:

> Whereas, within the County of Mendocino there are numerous examples of persons who totally disregard building as well as health and sanitation laws; and
>
> Whereas, for the health, safety, and welfare of the citizens of the County of Mendocino, it is essential that steps be taken immediately to combat the violators and to utilize all of the civil or criminal remedies;
>
> Now, therefore, be it resolved that a task force be created and that a representative from the building, health, and sheriff's departments join with a representative of the District Attorney's office to seek out the violators and pursue whatever remedies may be available to correct the violations.

"Citizens" were distinguished from "people" and "violators." Couldn't a violator be a citizen?

The notion that the victims of the task force were treated discriminantly was to become a central issue in the defense articulated by United Stand. More evidence than just the semantics of the Grand Jury resolution supported the contention that a lifestyle was under attack. One Grand Juror explicitly revealed his prejudice in excerpts from a letter to the supervisors:

> I was your first building inspection director and fought for years for compliance with this very same type of vociferous minority. They have always wanted to desecrate the most beautiful county in California.
>
> This same vociferous minority contributes little or nothing to the tax base of this county, and in many instances are a detriment to the county's enonomy.

> Who will determine where these substandard homes may be built? It will be either pure discrimination, or it will open up our county to every indigent in the United States.
>
> I am a third generation Mendocino County resident, and I beg of you not to allow these pressure groups to change our codes.

Chief Building Inspector Don Uhr outdid the Grand Juror for bigoted and untenable remarks. In a November, 1974, *New Times* article Uhr said:

> Suppose Mendocino does lower its building standards... every hippie and freak from all over the world is going to come storming here. They'll all be on welfare, or maybe just 50% on welfare. It would break the county.
>
> ...last week we had a fellow beat to death in one of the state parks on the coast. It could have been the motorcycle group or it could have been anyone. But when a guy professes peace and runs around with peace symbols on his collar, it don't mean he isn't going to beat your brains out if he gets a chance.[1]

These statements reflect the attitudes which gave rise to the task force.

Two sympathetic experts offered their resistance in those formative days of United Stand. One was Sim Van Der Ryn, a U.C. Berkeley professor of architecture. He told Mid-Mountain representatives the story of Canyon and gave them copies of his Owner-Built Home Resolution and his plans for a composting toilet. He put them in touch with the Housing Law Center at Berkeley and promised to provide health, sanitation, and architectural experts for their day in court.

Invaluable legal advice came from Carl Shapiro, an elderly and experienced attorney, who had successfully defended Marin County houseboat inhabitants from a land-fill, high-rise development planned for their harbor. Shapiro told United Stand organizers that their problem could not be defended from the posture of economic discrimination, for judges do not understand poverty. A defense built upon discriminate implementation had already been attempted and had failed. Furthermore, it would be inconsistent to demand that an unjust law be imposed on everyone equally.

The course chosen was to pursue all possible administrative remedies without lawyers, while conducting a campaign to educate the public to the motives, ideals, and lifestyle of the code victims. Deprecating stereotypes had to be dispelled in order to establish a broad base of support for their position. In the final analysis, judges and juries are influenced by public opinion. The Mid-Mountain people hoped to stall the judicial process to gain time to affect this opinion. A series of meetings was organized to share the stragegy. At this stage, United Stand—the organization and the name—was tentative. Confirmation came at a Ukiah meeting between task force representatives and concerned citizens.

Howdy!

The caricature logo of United Stand symbolizes the organization's pledge of "cooperation, education, and negotiation." "Howdy" is a comon figure in US literature.

The March 13, 1974, meeting was attended by over 200 people, including a sizeable number of long-time residents. The emerging spokespeople and primary organizers of United Stand—Anon Forrest, Saul Krimsley, John Pateros and Brent Walson—addressed the crowd, defining the problem as they saw it. Don Uhr and other task force representatives also spoke to the crowd. Uhr was cryptic: "Most of you have insoluable problems." The meeting marked the debut of United Stand and imparted the understanding that the political process must be used to gain relief. It became clear that many county bureaucrats (with the possible exception of Uhr) were not exuberant over the prospects of having to administer the supervisor's program. "Talk to the supervisors," United Stand was told.

Its ranks enhanced by 70 working volunteers, US organized itself into work committees. One group thoroughly studied the code and began a dialogue with the county administrators. Rapport was established with other task force victims throughout the county. Free spot messages on local radio stations were utilized. A bi-weekly newsletter became a regular feature on local counter-cultural newspaper. Candidates for public office were contacted, and those sympathetic to the cause were supported. A battery of lawyers, many of whom were living an alternative lifestyle, was assembled. A slideshow of owner-builder homes and a monologue explaining their point of view were developed. This presentation was to become the favorite medium by which this lifestyle was illustrated.

The task force itself did much to unify people behind United Stand's cause. It continued the taggings in other parts of the county and the tagees readily assembled under the US banner. Anon Forrest says about the public relations campaign and the continued taggings:

> We needed to be recognized as cohabitants of the county. Except for our hair and funky costumes, we're not very different from anyone else around here. We own the land we live on. We pay taxes on it. Of the 225 people at the church meeting, perhaps 70 were straights—old-time residents in town or retired people on little farms and ranches. Before the county officials showed up, we had about an hour to get our message across to them. We outlined what the problem was and what we thought the solutions were. We said that the problem was rooted in fear and misunderstanding. It was our paranoia. We'd left our image to their imagination, and we came out as Charlie Manson, drug addicts, and all kinds of other bad scenes they'd read about and seen on TV. Some of that started to change at the first meeting. Now a lot of those folks are with us. We owe the task force a lot—and this is not conciliatory bullshit. It forced us out of hiding and into a place in the community.[2]

Meanwhile, United Stand's crack team of lawyers threatened to file suit in Federal Court, alleging that the surreptitious task force taggings, the searches without warrants, the ensuing orders to demolish the homes, and the denial of the right to appeal—all violated the plaintiff's (United Stand's) constitutional rights to privacy and against unreasonable searches by government agents. Significantly, the potential suit clearly showed that the task force had violated the inspection and abatement procedures of the Uniform Building Code, the district attorney's Guidelines for Inspections, and Uhr's own Operation Guidelines for the Task Force. So much for administrators who "go by the book."

As United Stand prepared to meet with the supervisors, it had become, in two short months, a full-fledged organization touching many bases in Mendocino. It had filed suit against the county in Federal Court. Its operations were being subsidized by public support through donations and benefit activities. The supervisors *had* to listen.

On April 16, 1974, the presentation to the supervisors took place at the county courthouse. United Stand had prepared, along with the color slideshow, a tidy, professional 20-page booklet describing what US was, who it represented, a summary of its position, schematic drawings of alternative sanitation systems, and a proposal. US proposed that the board create a committee, composed of task force personnel and two supervisors, for the purposes of studying the violations and of making recommendations to the board "regarding administrative remedies for gaining the compliance of present violators." The supervisors had been offered a way out of the quagmire of their own creation, and they accepted unanimously. The Building and Land Use Review Committee, with the unfortunate but apropos acronym, BLUR, was formed.

The BLUR committee proved basically ineffectual. No member took the initiative necessary to implement solutions. On the issues of building and sanitation, all parties seemed content to fall back on the claim that it was not the responsibility of the county, since state-enacted codes were in question. United Stand attended the meetings diligently and offered intelligent input, but the taggings continued despite the on-going negotiations.

United Stand's desire to see the problem rectified locally was beginning to seem futile. The board of supervisors and the building department both disclaimed the power to interpretively modify the UBC. The district attorney said that it was his duty to carry on the abatement proceedings. By September, United Stand began to ask itself what to do when all reasonable measures of compliance and negotiation had expired. It had done its homework well in the nine months of its existence. It had learned the language of the various county departments and had offered methods by which alternative lifestyles could be embraced within the concepts and the letter of the codes. United Stand did the county's homework for it, but the people with authority remained impotent.

United Stand even spelled out county rights under state law by soliciting an Attorney General's Opinion which reaffirmed local

128

jurisdictional right to make code changes on the basis of "local topography, geography, or general condition." But, unhappily, only the district attorney was doing his job—145 outlaw builders had been cited, with the first tagees already enroute to court. Donald Uhr unwittingly offered a helpful suggestion. He told US to go the State Department of Housing and Community Development (the state-level guardians of the codes) since their concerns were a question of state law.

United Stand had made contact with the state government on one occasion. It had journeyed to Sacramento to describe its problems to Assemblyman Barry Keene and to Senator Peter Behr, both representing Mendocino County. Each legislator was sympathetic and helpful. Keene offered to introduce a spot bill if legislation proved necessary, but US was dedicated to local control. It avoided state intervention until it was certain that the county was going to continue to pass the buck.

Despite its leanings toward local self-determination, US sounded out candidates for state office on the issues it was raising. On October 12, 1974, US met in Ukiah with Edmund G. (Jerry) Brown,

Anon Forrest of United Stand frowns at a sign on the entrance door to the California State Capitol Building. A government building not up to code can get by with an "Enter at Your Own Risk" sign. Why not an owner-built home?

who was on the campaign trail to the governor's office. Brown was asked for his views on housing and uniformity. He answered that urban housing had to follow the guidelines of economics, ecology, energy, but that "the cabin up in the hills" should not come under state-mandated uniformity. US informed him that the UBC precluded the cabin in the hills. Brown couldn't understand this, but asked to be kept informed of US activities.

On April 2, 1975, just three months after his inauguration as Governor of the State of California, Jerry Brown was to hear the United Stand story in full. As the first defendants were about to go to trial in Mendocino for the heinous crime of building their homes without a permit, US was granted a late-night interview with the governor. The slideshow was presented and their problems defined for him. He urged US to submit a bill which he said he would sign, provided the bill was no longer than one page. "This administration doesn't read anything longer than one page," the governor said, taking a poke at the notorious California bureaucracy. United Stand was dumb-founded—seemingly it had finally arrived at the place where the buck stopped passing.

California newspapers flippantly treated Jerry Brown's support of United Stand issues as "the governor coming out for outhouses." But, for these United Stand delegates, Brown's responsiveness helped restore their faith in government.

130

United Stand did not author a bill, because a tactical decision was reached to seek administrative remedies on the state level. With a willing governor, there was no problem establishing the remedial procedure.

A pilot project was begun to study the situation of rural owner-builders and to recommend a new and less restrictive article to the state housing law. The committee to conduct the study was called the Class K Steering Committee—"Class K" coming from a US proposal to add a new classification to the UBC's existing A-J categories of structures.

At the time of this writing, the Class K Steering Committee has had four meetings, and it appears that a new "owner-builder" regulation will evolve in California. It won't be a panacea to the big brother syndrome in government, and it won't solve the need for alternative sewage systems—a major problem area for owner-

In the first three United Stand cases, the defendants either had their cases dismissed or were acquitted by a jury trial.

builders. It could, however, serve to take the heat off owner-builders of simple, ecological dwellings. Perhaps, in time, the UBC *will* evolve into a code of one page!

The first court cases of United Stand members have fortunately resulted in acquittals. Brilliant legal counsel by United Stand attorney, Barry Vogel, and the one-year statute of limitations combined to result in US victories in the first three cases. Unhappily, the judge ruled as irrelevant arguments on Due Process and Equal Protection, lifestyle, and geographical and topographical considerations.

United Stand is confident that its hard work will be justified. An owner-builder amendment to the housing code is a first step. Adding a page of law to the existing volumes does not solve the problem, Anon Forrest acknowledges, but she says assuredly that in the end "reason will prevail."

United Stand chapters have formed in other California counties as a demonstration of support for the right to build. Each group has sought to influence local implementation of the uniform codes.

Dean's House

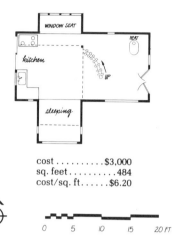

```
cost . . . . . . . . . $3,000
sq. feet . . . . . . . . . 484
cost/sq. ft . . . . . . $6.20
```

```
0     5     10    15    20 FT
```

Description

This little two-story frame structure sits on a level spot excavated from the southern slope of a fairly steep hill. The large space on the main floor has a kitchen at the west end, a water bed alcove to the south, and a window seat to the north. A twisted log ladder leads to a sleeping loft above.

A concrete slab, with copper tubing for a future radiant heating system, provides a floor surface in the main space, while the appendages to the north and south rest on post-and-joist systems. The conventionally framed walls are shingled on the exterior and sheathed with boards on the interior. The north-facing roof surfaces are covered with translucent corrugated fiberglass, and the south-facing surfaces are insulated. These insulated roof surfaces (after Rex Roberts) consist of 1" sheathing nailed over the rafters followed by two air spaces backed with double-sided foil, another air-space, and finally, aluminum-ribbed roofing. The doors and most of the windows were salvaged from dumpsters in San Francisco. Dean made some leaded glass windows as well as some ceramic tiles for the kitchen counter.

There is no electricity, so Dean cooks with gas and illuminates with old-fashioned gas lights. He heats with a combination of gas and wood. There is an uphill spring which provides water during the winter months, but in the summer, water must be carried uphill from an old well. The kitchen sink drains into a leach pit, and there is an outhouse about 200 yards downhill.

Comments

Dean was working in the city as a graphic designer when he began to think seriously about moving to the country. He looked in the want-ads

for rural property and, on an impulse, bought 28 acres located a few hours from the city. There was a small shack on his new place, so Dean, being unemployed, moved in.

For the next couple of years he occasionally returned to the city in order to earn a living, but he eventually decided to build a studio so he could work at home.

A neighbor excavated a level spot and, after weeks of additional labor, Dean poured his concrete slab. He usually worked alone, so he realized he would have to work diligently to get the building ready for winter. As he was proceeding, he realized that his studio-to-be was developing into a place more comfortable than his present living quarters. He therefore decided to make his studio into a house. Favorable weather allowed him to enclose the structure before winter, and he has been living in (and working on) his house ever since.

He has plans for a fireplace which will heat and circulate water through the slab floor. He has also leveled a spot to the west of the house where he plans to add a greenhouse and a bathroom.

12. Reform

The debate about what place owner-built homes should occupy within the context of housing codes has ranged from the extremist arguments of demolition-minded officials to the disclaimer by recalcitrant builders of any legitimate government interest in their homes. Typically, in spite of one's point of view, the solution will probably be found somewhere between these two extremes. The authors believe people should be given the maximum amount of freedom to build homes for themselves in the interest of low-impact technology, of resourceful economics, and of the preservation of Constitutional liberty.

Thanks to the publicity given it by the Rodale Press, *Mother Earth News* and other back-to-the-land media, we now know the hassle between owner-builders and code-enforcing agencies to be a nation-wide phenomenon. Mendocino County has reportedly spent from one-quarter to one-half million tax dollars attempting to abate owner-built homes. Mendocino has become a model for how *not* to pursue code-enforcement. As a result, some counties have toyed with the idea of making code violations a civil, rather than a criminal, affair. We hope more will be learned from Mendocino's example than how to prosecute owner-built homes more efficiently.

Building codes are the result of many years of evolution, which makes instantaneous reform unlikely. United Stand was created in an *ad hoc* situation of having to defend its constituency from the imminent destruction of their homes. US proposals were often stop-gap measures, yet they were effective attempts to interject owner-builder concepts into bureaucratic programming. Basically, the three major areas which US has sought to influence are building, sanitation and land-use.

BUILDING. The code failures section of this book depicts some specific defects of building codes as they pertain to low-cost owner-built homes. Creating a new classification of dwellings within the code which waives many of the urban, contractor-built dwelling requirements, is probably the best method of legitimatizing the homes built by owner-builders. A distinction must be made between homes built for profit and homes built for personal shelter, and between rural homes as opposed to urban homes. Class K housing is the first attempt to institute these concepts and is imminent only because of the indefatigable political organizing done by United Stand.

An amendment to the building code is difficult to secure. For example, the International Conference of Building Officials, author of the western-based UBC, is virtually unapproachable by the layperson. ICBO has a procedure for code change recommendations, but it is costly and is geared to businessmen seeking acceptance of new, marketable construction products or methods. Sweeping substantive reform is not likely to be gained by non-commercial individuals appealing to ICBO's sensibilities.

Another avenue for amending the UBC is through legislative action, but this route is obviously limited. Writing one's elected representatives is a nice notion but, in reality, is a difficult way to gain relief from a problem. Even when blessed with a responsive state representative, pushing a bill through a state legislature means running the gauntlet of high-pressure politics, lobbying, and high finance. For this reason, United Stand sought state-level *administrative* remedies—possible in part because Jerry Brown is a unique governor.

Appeals within the code system itself are also difficult. The local building appeals board, provided by the UBC, is almost universally stacked with contractors and engineers who approach the problem from an industrial point of view. Lay membership on the board is rare. In California, the state equivalent to a local appeals board is the State Housing Commission, also constituted by professionals. This commission has administrative powers to effect code changes but was avoided by United Stand, because it was populated by unsympathetic hold-overs from the Reagan administration. (Again, the politics of building your home!)

Despite the difficulties of influencing a code change, a Class K type of revision does seem to be the most equitable way for the code to regain a measure of legitimacy and for owner-built homes to be legally sanctioned. A Class K type of resolution should waive the superfluous requirements of current dwelling classification; which means the government should limit its concern to basic matters of public health, safety and environmental impact—not matters of private design, construction and convenience. An amendment of this kind could include the following requisites:

1) The structure may have a limited projected lifespan (perhaps 10-15 years.).

2) The building shall be constructed by the property owner or his agent for the owner's use or for people related by blood or law.

3) Permits shall be required only for initial construction or major structural alterations, not for minor alternations or repair.

4) Permit fees will be either *waived entirely* or based upon actual value of the structure.

5) The structure shall be built in areas designated by local determination.

How long should a house last? Without care, a code-built house will deteriorate beyond repair in fewer than 50 years while its foundation will last thousands.

A special classification of this sort would be unnecessary if local building officials would use common sense when exercising discretionary powers such as those granted under Section 106 of the UBC. An official using common sense could grant variances to the code on the basis of local economics, population density, geography, climate, or community compatibility, without sacrificing health or safety. Allowing a building official to exercise judgement is necessary for local problem-solving, since a code cannot account for every conceivable situation. But Section 106 also creates the possibility for a local official to act upon whim and arbitrary fiat. This is precisely why United Stand has sought statutory change which explicitly deals with owner-builders.

Another possibility for reform would be the adoption of a local ordinance, setting criteria for owner-built homes. While attempting to determine whether the state or local government had jurisdiction over the code, United Stand discovered that a nearby county had passed a resolution allowing vacation, hunting, and camp cabins to be built under the Group J (storage sheds) classification of the UBC. The resolution waives all structural requirements, minimum numbers of rooms, room sizes, ceiling heights, sanitation facilities and running water. The ordinance is based on a point system which considers the lot size, altitude, type of access road, population density, terrain, etc. Each consideration merits a different value, to be multiplied by the points assigned to the factors under consideration. Permits are issued for a cabin which earns a minimum number of points. A county could pass a similar ordinance pertaining to permanently-occupied owner-built dwellings.

The ordinance cited above showed that a county could creatively apply the UBC to its situation. This county is mountainous, sparsely-settled, and cabins are commonplace; so the government accomodated the code to that reality. This example also showed that the state would only intervene if safety were grossly sacrificed by a local code amendment.

Mendocino's 1970 General Plan (under the housing section) determined that "the greatest need is for housing for the low and medium income families." It deduced that private industry could not possibly meet the demand because of the high costs of land, labor, and materials. The low income families represented by

138

Non-code houses, like pre-code houses, will be bought and sold. Potential buyers could be supplied with a list of those parts of the house not built to standard.

United Stand solved their own housing problems, only to face abatement by county administrators. When confronted by public outcry, these administrators claimed to be powerless to change the codes. This is the lowest form of governmental response.

Another question raised in the debate on substandard structures concerns consumer protection. If lower standards are offered for owner-built homes, then how will the safety of eventual buyers or renters be assured? Two possible solutions emerged during the debate: 1) an assemblyman suggested writing into the property deed that the building is 'Class K," "substandard" or whatever term applied, informing the buyer of what he was getting; 2) a Mendocino social and economic planner suggested that plans be submitted by the builder, that the building department evaluate the plans and insure that they are followed, and that future buyers be required to review the plans and read the evaluation. Certainly, these solutions pose no greater threat to the consumer than those faced by auto purchasers when they drive on freeways.

United Stand explored other possibilities for reform such as the creation of "architectural free zones," areas conditionally designated as outside the UBC's jurisdiction. This idea never gained acceptance, because it ran contrary to the type of control on which the UBC is predicated. At this stage a Class K amendment, allowing people to build homes within their means, seems to be the most workable compromise.

LAND USE. Local planning and zoning follow state guidelines for land utilization. Counties apply the state's classification descriptions to their geographical area. Planning and zoning concepts are usually based on the predicate of a single dwelling for a nuclear family on a specifically defined lot. The trend toward co-operative living has produced "extended families" of non-blood "relatives" who live communally in one or more dwellings, or in a loosely-defined community. Even in areas where neo-homesteaders have bought land independently, familiarity and similarity of purpose tend to effectively erase property lines. The expression of co-operative community often runs contrary to local zoning ordinances, thus creating an illegal situaion.

One example of this is Ananda Co-operative Community in Nevada County, CA. Ananda is a large, well-organized religious community, enonomically sustained through religious retreats, individual crafts, and small businesses. Ananda has legally existed as an organized camp, but its growth and development of community schools have moved it into a situation devoid of land-use definition. In real life Ananda thrives, but the legal void in which it now exists has caused county authorities to issue stop-work orders on further community development.

With regard to individual owner-builders, United Stand has lobbied for zoning changes which would allow building permits to be obtained for more than one dwelling per parcel to allow "clustering" of dwellings, without a requirement for separate parcels or for changes to existing lot lines. This cluster concept would allow a community to develop and to build homes, irrespective of property lines. If one parcel, for example, has an abundance of water but poor access, and a contiguous parcel has the reverse situation, the two land-owners could both build on the accessible parcel and develop a common water system on the other. This is a reasonable response to the state-sanctioned land development practice of carving land into large parcels without regard to water sources, usability, etc.

SANITATION. Inasmuch as this subject requires a lengthy treatment, we have placed it in a previous chapter.

A discussion of code reform would be incomplete without exploring further the necessity for input from owner-builders into the political process which regulates their activities. Government is a two-way process, involving the mutually interdependent opposites of governors and the governed. Owner-builders have been, to this date, naively immersed in their idyllic vision, while assuming the American social-political framework will stretch to accomodate new cultural forms. In a sense, they have played political ostrich.

The experience of United Stand is healthy from the point of view that it forced the new homesteaders of Mendocino "out of the hills" into the community. The potential for reforming the uniform codes is deeply-rooted in the ability of government bureaucracy to respond to people's changing needs and in the ability of people to articulate those needs. United Stand is the best known example of

owner-builders politicizing their lives in an effort to participate in the political process.

It is important that people take the initiative to explain their alternative lifestyles. As United Stand witnessed, there is a danger in leaving this information to the imaginations of the media, the average citizen, or the authorities. Too often, owner-builders are forced to operate defensively against spurious attacks by uninformed or abusive authority. It is easier to communicate on neutral ground than with one's back to the wall.

Even more important to the cause of improving the condition of owner-builders is the willingness of building officials to respond to their needs. Most building departments have the capability of providing the assistance needed by owner-builders. These departments are staffed by former contractors, architects, and engineers, and they possess a wealth of construction knowledge which could be shared. This sharing could be in the form of assistance and instruction to the department's customers.

Most owner-builders have never designed or built a house and, therefore, they make fundamental mistakes in these disciplines. Basic design and construction information is available from many sources (see chapters 7 & 8),but inexperienced owner-builders are often incapable of integrating this information. Indeed, the number of construction concepts which must be considered simultaneously can overwhelm them. Owner-builders make errors in judgement, because they must make many decisions based on unfamiliar and incomplete information.

The best solution to the owner-builders' dilemma would be for them to have permanent access to an experienced house-builder— one who would serve as a resource person for design and construction concepts, who would evaluate and insure the completeness of these concepts, and who would provide instruction when requested. A logical place for this builder-advocate to abide would be in the community building department. This is plausible only if the term "civil service" still has meaning.

The advent of an in-department consultant could only occur simultaneously with a transformation of attitude in building departments themselves. They must stop thinking of themselves only as an *enforcer of regulations*. They need to begin thinking of themselves also as a *provider of public service*. All builders—

owner-builders and contractors alike—need personalized service.

The implications of such a change are far-reaching. The building department's relationship with its clients would be completely transformed. Builders would cease viewing inspectors with suspicion and resentment. The building official would be thought of as someone other than an all-powerful autocrat. Candor would replace deceit and, in this atmosphere, the owner-builder would be able to come out of hiding and into a respectable place in the construction community.

Reinstating public service as its primary function would greatly benefit the building department. No longer would builder and inspector be antagonists. Indeed, they would become protagonists. As a by-product, building department personnel would find new meaning in their jobs. Their work would become more challenging, and the rewards immensely greater. No longer would they have to serve exclusively as the bureaucratic functionaries of a regulatory agency.

The "reformed" building department could provide booklets on fundamental aspects of construction. Inasmuch as the plumbing and electrical codes are unintelligible to the layperson, enforcement agencies could dispense simple booklets explaining how to wire and plumb a house to code specifications. Similarly, a booklet could be proferred indicating basic structural requirements, illustrating simple design concepts, and showing one how to prepare plans required by the building department. A resident designer-consultant could provide information pertinent to local building conditions—soil types, snow loads, insulation factors, etc. Consultants could offer more than raw structural knowledge; they could tender design suggestions as well.

This book does not offer a blue-print for reform which will instantly transform bureaucrats into civil servants and laws into embodiments of wisdom. The issues involved in code philosophy are very complex. Meaningful reform of building departments must come from within the departments themselves—with a little prodding from an informed public.

We believe, like United Stand, that people *are* the government, and that only through affirmative political action may the people's will be felt. The struggle of people to save their homes from government condemnation—homes which, in most cases, are "unsafe" only because they have been defined as such—is indicative of the tough road ahead toward responsive government. A Class K housing amendment is merely the battle—not the war.

The skeleton of this 22 foot high dome is made of automobile chassis, salvaged from abandoned cars which used to litter the owner-builders' 20 acre farm. After functional car doors and windows were set in place, the structure was filled with a huge polyethylene film bag and sprayed from the outside with polyurethane foam.

Lawrence and Hattie's Barn

workshop | living | bedroom
HEAT
kitchen
REF

cost $3,600
sq. feet 1,728
cost/sq. ft. $2.08

0   5   10   15   20 FT.

Description

This two-story, 24'x36' building sits on a hill at the edge of a clearing. The entrance is on the uphill side. The space is organized into three 12'x24' bays, the central one being two feet taller on the main floor than the other two. Two of the bays on the main floor are used as temporary living space. There is a bathroom which divides a kitchen from a bedroom, and these spaces open directly onto the tall central bay which has a ten-foot sliding door at its south end. Clerestory windows between the two ceiling heights admit light from the second floor. The third bay on the main floor is a workshop, and the entire second floor is used for storage.

The building is modeled after the traditional post-and-beam barn, but it is built exclusively of new materials (except for windows and doors). Four 36-foot frames are the substance of the building. The posts and beams of the frames are joined with mortice and tenon joints, and the knee braces are let-in and pegged. There is not a single nail holding the frames together, but the rest of the building

is all nailed to them. Two-by-fours, nailed horizontally and diagonally to the outside of the frames, provide nailing for the 1x12 cedar siding and brace the building as well. Built-up plates span from frame to frame supporting the shake roof.

The walls in the living space are covered with 1x6 tongue and groove cedar. They are insulated with a layer of foil on the outside face of the 1½" dead air space. The ceiling and floor are insulated with rigid insulation. The living space is heated with a wood heater. Water is pumped from a cistern fed by a spring. The toilet empties into a sump, and the other waste water drains onto the ground.

Comments

This is Lawrence and Hattie's second owner-built home. After three years in their first house, they decided they wanted more land closer to town. They sold the house and acquired 30 acres. Their plan for the new place was to quickly and inexpensively construct a large barn which would include a temporary living space, a workshop, and a substantial amount of storage. Their idea was to provide themselves a comfortable place to life, a place to work, and a place to stockpile materials while they designed and built their future home.

They had learned from the experience of building their first house that they did not want to have to build their next one quickly. They wanted to be able to take their time in choosing the site and designing their new house, and they wanted to be able to build it unhurriedly, without any pressure to make compromises. This would mean that the house would not be finished until three to five years hence, which is what ultimately led them to the barn/temporary house idea.

Since Lawrence and Hattie were planning to occupy their barn only temporarily, they did not plan to install a septic system. The possibility of applying for a dwelling permit was, therefore, automatically eliminated. They did, however, apply for an agricultural building permit which allowed them to construct the building legally without having to worry about hiding it. This way, should they be discovered and prosecuted after they had moved in, the worst they could be accused of would be the illegal occupation of an agricultural building. Without the permit, they could have been accused of constructing an illegal dwelling.

They built a road to the site, bought a travel trailer, and arranged for "temporary" power. Some friends had been persuaded to help, and the four of them began construction. Six weeks later, when their friends left, the shell of the barn was complete. For the next six weeks, Lawrence and Hattie were at work finishing the building. They hung the doors and windows, installed the plumbing and electrical systems, applied the interior walls and ceilings, and installed the heater. They moved in at the end of October, about three months after they had begun.

Almost a year has passed since they moved in, and Lawrence and Hattie are still quite comfortable in their temporary quarters. They wish it had a private space so they could carry on independent activities without disturbing one another, but they are comfortable enough to postpone building their house in favor of smaller projects—clearing land, putting in a garden, building a chicken house, a goat shed, a wood storage shed, etc. Although they say they are comfortable, they are still looking forward to their permanent house.

13. Evasion

A recent United Nations statistic may be interpreted as follows: if the world's population were represented by a community of 1,000 people, 800 of them would be "living in shacks or mud huts." Sixty of them, representing the population of the U.S., would receive one-half of the total world income, but fifty of these sixty U.S. residents would be living on only 1% of this country's land. In other words, the vast majority of housing for the world's inhabitants fails to meet minimum safe-and-sanitary standards, and the majority of U.S.dwellings are located in congested areas, requiring some form of building regulation. The authors are faced with the dillemma of advocating building freedom for those owner-builders living on the rural 99% of the land, while not wanting to exclude the urban majority who live on the remaining 1% of the land. Urban owner-builders need relief from oppressive building regulations, as well.

Building code evasion is the common denominator unifying urban and rural owner-builders. Curiously, the techniques developed to evade code regulations have become the common-ground communication between owner-builders everywhere. Most owner-builders interviewed by the authors seem proud and eager to elaborate their favorite evasive tactics.

In this chapter, we will elaborate some of these important evasive techniques. It should be pointed out, however, that when we describe how others avoid building regulations by breaking the law we view the process as provisional to long-overdue code reform legislation. This particular chapter is written for those growing numbers of owner-builders who cannot wait for code reform measures to evolve. The anticipation of belated code reform does little to alleviate one's immediate need for housing. We justify code evasion on this basis only, and we anticipate that readers will choose that method of evasion which best fits their circumstances.

At the outset, it is important for the outlaw builder to understand the basic machinations of the bureaucratic code-enforcing structure and something about the mentality of those who perpetrate it. In our society, there is probably no better example of bureaucracy-at-work than that which is found in the building department. Webster defines bureaucracy as "a system of administration marked by lack of initiative and flexibility, by indifference to human need or public opinion, and by a tendency to defer decisions to superiors or to impede action with red tape." The building department is all of these things and more. Its operation is generally slow and cumbersome. Management is often inundated with paperwork-without-purpose. New information about building methods and materials tends to decrease the decision-making capacity, because diversity and newness confuse the bureaucratic system. As the building department gains authority, its administrative functions increase and it becomes more difficult to manage. The establishment of routine and specialization of function ensue, and specialization becomes synonymous with authority. Finally, the original purpose of the building department changes from one of *performance* to that of *control*.

A similar evolutionary process takes place in the formation of the bureaucratic field worker, the building inspector. To maintain the high degree of efficiency expected of his office, the building inspector must work within a well-defined hierarchy. He accepts a division-of-labor and acknowledges authority; in fact, he symbolizes authority. His work responsibility is carefully prescribed and channeled, and he must remain within boundaries.

A highly evolved building inspector-type expresses little person-to-person *directness* in his relations with builders. His professional relationships are mediated through a higher, third-person authority. It is little wonder that the average building inspector relies heavily on the orthodox version of the code. If he applies reason to a building situation, he may fear over-stepping his authority and, subsequently, opening himself to charges of favoritism. Yet, when interpreting the code verbatim, he is certain to run into inconsistencies. Orthodoxy, of course, is an armor plate for insecure authoritarians. (A handbook for training managers for General Electric contains the admonition, "Never say anything controversial.")

It is the bureaucratic power drive that makes the building regulatory system most vulnerable. The building codes which "authorize" entry by building inspectors into any structure or premises distend building department power, compromising citizen's rights. Camara challenged the right of a building inspector to enter his San Francisco premises without a search warrant. He was arrested for violation of the housing code, but his right to refuse entry was upheld by the U.S. Supreme Court. Writing for the Court, Justice White maintained that searches for housing violations are significant intrusions on the privacy and security of individuals—interests protected by the Fourth Amendment which guarantees homes against arbitrary invasions by government officials. The Fourth Amendment also assures that warrants can be issued only upon specific instance, "describing the place to be

To reach this non-code owner-built home, a building inspector would either have to cross a 100 ft. suspension bridge with no handrails or go through the ravine.

searched, and the persons or things to be seized." It was pointed out in the Camara case that neither the code of the City of San Francisco nor the code of the State of California provided sufficient authority to issue a search warrant for the inspection of Camara's premises. (Actually, there is only one state, New Jersey, which authorizes the issuance of a search warrant specifically for the purpose of detecting housing code violations—apparently in violation of the U.S. Constitution.)

Evidence obtained by virtue of an unlawful search and seizure is inadmissable in court. That is, any evidence obtained during an illegal search would itself be illegal. "It is not admissable to do a great right by doing a little wrong...It is not sufficient to do justice by obtaining a proper result by irregular or improper means." (Miranda vs State of Arizona, 1966) Because it must operate on a tenuous constitutional foundation, it is in the building department's best interest to maintain a low profile.

Building code enforcement agencies generally make an effort to keep maverick home builders in at least partial compliance with code regulations. But, if an existing structure is found to be substandard or built without a permit, it is usually not condemned for demolition. The building department must consider the expense of bringing offenders to court and the effect that confrontation will have on its bureaucratic routine. In cases where the proposed construction will not comply with the codes, it is generally advisable for the home builder to take the initiative to build first and face possible legal repercussions later.

Chances of detection by the building department can be minimized if a few common sense precautions are observed. As already pointed out, the bureaucratically-oriented building department is not purposely seeking code violators. Seek-and-report helicopters observed hovering over the countryside are most likely sponsored by the local tax assessor's office or the county sheriff, not by the building department. In sophisticated jurisdiction, however, these county departments may communicate amongst themselves.

Practically all the information about code-violating structures is received by the building department from individual informers. Hostile neighbors comprise the largest source. Understandably, people sometimes feel threatened with the appearance nearby of an unorthodox owner-built home. Complaints come also from

150

people who transfer their own animosity for the building department to owner-builders who seem to be violating the code with impunity.

There are other sources of detection beside that offered by vindictive neighbors. Electric power companies are often closely associated with the building department. Any alteration of service supply or observable changes in building structure may be reported by the monthly meter reader. In many sections of the country, electric service will not be installed by the power company until the appropriate building, electrical and sanitation permits have been issued.

In one community known to the authors, refuse disposal workers are encouraged to report building violations encountered in the process of trash collecting. To avoid detection, it behooves one to maintain a low profile and to live in an isolated area, not visible from a public thoroughfare or neighboring houses, without commercial utilities, and without community services.

Most often, a building site with these qualities is not available. In most instances, one must employ techniques that confront the building codes and, simultaneously, avoid ensuing legal repercussions. The universal method for evading building regulation is to build in stages, at times when the authorities are least apt to detect activity. The illustration below shows how an Indian shopkeeper develops his illegal street-shop by slowly, each night, improving and expanding his premises.

Squatting by stages. The art of the game is never to make a move which is so drastic as to attract attention.
—Architectural Design 8/73

Greek squatters, living beyond Athenian suburbs, similarly use evening, off-duty, and holiday hours to erect their owner-built structures. In his book *Shelter and Society*, Paul Oliver tells how they utilize every available moment to surreptitiously work on their homes. When sirens are heard in the nearby city, these people feverishly work on their dwellings, knowing that the sirens signify police involvement with other matters and that authorities are unlikely to appear for a housing bust.[1]

Owner-builders in this country have been known to preassemble wall, floor, and roof panels for instant erection on weekends or holidays. This is an especially viable technique where single room additions are desired. Another idea is to install a high privacy fence around publicly exposed portions of one's house to deter neighborhood snoopers.

On occasion, it may be necessary to co-operate to some degree with the building department—for instance, when a building permit is mandatory for an electrical service installation. Under

Ernie and Jeanette obtained an electrical permit and wired their non-code house. But, when the power company saw that the house had no foundation or septic system, they demanded a $3,000 installation charge. Not to be outsmarted, Ernie built a small code-approved agricultural building next to an existing power pole. After this building was hooked up free of charge, he ran a line from it to a 12-volt system in the house.

152

these circumstances, different methods of evasion and diversion may have to be employed against the building authority. Countless numbers of "barns" have been built in code-enforced but agriculturally-exempt areas. These "barns" and "storage sheds" are later converted to habitable dwellings—after the electrical power hook-up has been made. (See pages 66, 74, and 144)

Another imaginative solution is to apply for a permit to cover the most rudimentary, minimum-sized shelter acceptable by law. Under UBC regulations this consists of a 150 square foot structure:

> Section 1407b. Every dwelling unit shall have at least one room which shall have not less than 120 square feet of superficial floor area. Every room which is used for both cooking and living or both living and sleeping purposes shall have not less than 150 square feet of superficial floor area.

After the final inspection, the "approved" structure can become the nucleus for a wide range of agriculturally-exempted additions. A grape arbor may become an outdoor summer living room. A greenhouse may make an excellent indoor winter living room. Hay lofts may become sleeping lofts, and an agricultural food processing center may become a kitchen. To qualify under an agricultural exemption, according to the UBC, one must have at least three

Code approved core unit.

acres of land and structures must be located more than 50 feet from the property line. This is an important consideration to keep in mind when choosing a parcel of land upon which to build.

The drawing below ilustrates one manner in which it may be possible to develop a complete homestead living unit from a basic, code-approved core. The result is a space-sufficient, efficient, and economically-built environment. Paradoxically, this scheme is generated by the code, itself.

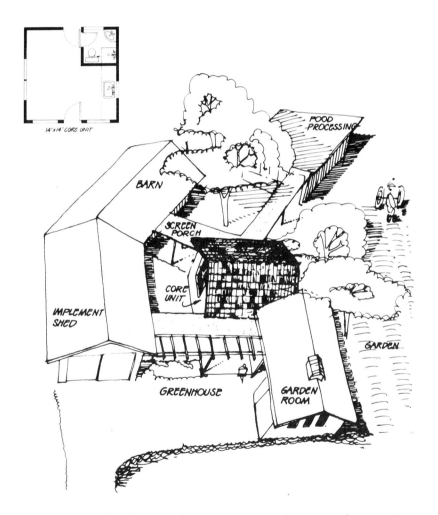

14'x14' CORE UNIT

Agricultural building development around code approved core unit.

In a sense, it is unfortunate that most innovative owner-builders have chosen to evade the building codes. By evading the codes, they also evade the fundamental question of whether a person has a right to build a house for himself in any way he sees fit as long as he doesn't endanger the health or safety of others. If this question is ever to be answered, there must be confrontations in the courts between owner-builders and the uniform codes.

Mrs. Harry Bewick (seated) lives south of Dublin in a standard garden greenhouse which she bought secondhand for $70 in 1960. She is a hearty woman who has a daily swim in the river, sleeps mostly out of doors, and keeps warm in cold weather by putting on more clothes. She maintains her privacy from snoopers by plugging in the tea kettle.

—drawn from Architectural Design photo

Slim's House

cost $11,500
sq. feet 3,500
cost/sq. ft. $3.30

MAIN FLOOR

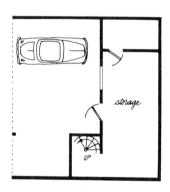

GROUND FLOOR

Description

This three story house was built almost entirely from the remains of an old saw mill, locally quarried basalt rock, and locally cut cedar logs. The ground floor, consisting of carport and storage areas, has a slab floor and concrete stem walls which support the western half of the floors above. The main floor, which contains all the living space of the house, is on two levels. The lower-level living room has floors made of 4x12 timbers laid flat and spiked to supporting girders; the main level has floors made of 3x12 timbers. The walls of the north and east sides of this floor are all of basalt rock one foot thick. These are the walls which include the fireplaces of both the living room and master bedroom. The remainder of the walls of this floor and other floors are standard stud walls. The ceilings of the main floor consist of 2x12 planks laid flat and covered with tarpaper. The ceiling and walls of this floor are insulated with fiberglass batts as this is the only floor which is heated. Each room is provided with its own electric hideaway heater with in individual thermostat.

The attic floor consists of 2x4 joists covered with ¾" plywood. The ceiling of the attic, which is the roof of the building, is made of 2x8 tongue and groove decking covered on the outside with hand-split cedar shakes. All three floors are connected by means of a circular steel staircase. Water is from a well, and sewage flows into a septic system.

Comments

This is a truly remarkable house. It is impressive for its size, for its low cost, for the massiveness of its construction, and especially for the effort that went into building it. Slim is a lawyer, a big man who says he "gets his jollies" from hard physical work. When one sees the house he built in 2½ years during his spare time, it is apparent he has been a very happy man.

As a start, he bought a section of an abandoned lumber mill for $400. He dismantled it and hauled the huge timbers and other lumber to his building site. He estimates that he salvaged 50,000 board feet of lumber from the old mill—enough for 90% of the lumber he needed to build the house, with some left over. He hand-placed about 100 tons of rock to build the exterior walls and the

fireplaces. For the roof, he bought $27 worth of cedar timber from the Bureau of Land Management. He logged the trees himself, cut them into bolts, and split them into shakes using a froe and mallet. This $27 worth of BLM timber gave him enough shakes to cover his entire roof (35 squares), plus he had 10 squares extra and 100 ten-foot posts.

Unfortunately, Slim never got to finish his house. He was about 85% complete when he discovered traces of boron in his water supply. He is very interested in rhodydendron hybridization experiments, and boron is detrimental to these plants. Because of this, he decided to move. He has bought more land where he is starting to build another house.

WEST ELEVATION

14. The Future

The right to build one's own home without government interference suggests few, if any, profound implications. Certainly a book-length treatment should not be required to establish such a basic tenent. But today, owner-builders symbolically represent the tip of an iceberg: they are taking a stand for freedom that will affect the rights of every citizen, even those residing in urban apartments who have no intention of ever building their own house. The iceberg is sinking; soon it will be too late for individuals to proclaim and insure their rights under Constitutional law. We will all go together when we go. The dilemma was spelled out by Winston Churchill when he said:

> If you will not fight for right when you can easily win without bloodshed, if you will not fight when your victory will be sure and not too costly, you may come to the moment when you will have to fight with all the odds against you and only a precarious chance of survival. There may be even a worse fate. You may have to fight when there is no hope of victory, because it is better to perish than live as slaves.

The loss of the right to build one's own home accompanies the general breakdown of the private sector of our economy. A coalition of government and big business is precipitating this breakdown. As this reciprocal action between big business and government proceeds, bureaucracy expands. In the shuffle, it is the individual who loses. Work becomes mechanized, de-personalized, and routinized. Life becomes regulated by the business-government coalition.

Consider the effect on our free enterprise system of one recently instigated government regulatory agency. A stack of regulations, totaling seventeen feet in height, enumerates the Departments of Labor's Occupational Safety and Health Administration's (OSHA) coverage of every "workplace or environment where work is performed." Any workplace can be inspected by an OSHA Compliance Officer without prior notice. Since the agency was created in 1970, an average of 75% of all workplaces visited have been found to be in violation of agency standards. Three million dollars in fines were collected in the first year alone.[1]

The OSHA experience confirms a prediction that James Burnham made in his book, The Managerial Revolution, published over thirty years ago. Burnham felt that a new ruling class of appointed managers were destined to replace elected representatives. Managerial rule will occur through federal ownership and control, he said. Regulation is the principal concept of comtemporary social and political thought. Regulations are rampant—from the economy to building, land use, and environmental protection.

Many would have us believe that the controls and regulations imposed on us are conspiratorial in nature, deliberately created by those in power. "Phony" food and fuel shortages are cited as the conditioning used to force the people to accept a planned and computerized society. Conspiracy or not, deterioration of our environment has led to massive government control in the guise of the Environmental Protection Agency. The environment has not improved, but regulations have proliferated. The conspiracy theme appeared again in 1973 when the President's Commission on Population and the American Future suggested that 64 million people be moved to a few major "development centers." Whether these controls are deliberately orchestrated by a new managerial ruling class is not really the issue. The fact is that oppressive controls are happening; they are happening now, and they are happening fast!

The type of government regulation mentioned here probably had its origin during the Depression. The Roosevelt Planners knew that their social policies could not be implemented as long as small divisions of state and county government existed. Constitutionally, the county remains the most basic and potentially powerful seat of government in the United States. Only the county sheriff has the legal right to mobilize the citizenry into a posse comitatus. By "regionalizing" the nation, small divisional county governments as well as state governments could be effectively eliminated in favor of an *appointed* regional adminstrator, responsible only to Washington, D.C.

Roosevelt's plan was not acceptable. It was not until the Nixon Administration that the planners' approach was slipped to the American people. As Nixon himself declared on the 17th of September, 1973: "Land use control is perhaps the most pressing environmental issue before the nation." By signing a series of Executive Orders, Nixon wrote into law a modernized version of Roosevelt's regional land use plan.

An Executive Order was originally intended to be only an administrative order from the President to his cabinet officers. Nixon used the privilege to make laws by edict, subverting representative government by by-passing Congress. He did this under the guise of "national emergency". Once an Executive Order becomes published in the Federal Register, it becomes the law of the land.

Nixon signed two dictatorial orders into law: EO 11490 and EO 11647. The first directive assigns "Emergency Preparedness Functions to Federal Departments and Agencies."[2] It is a consolidation of a dozen or more Executive Orders from previous administrations, providing for implementation "by an order or directive issued by the President in any national emergency type of situation." Under the guise of a "national emergency," the Executive Branch can comandeer all communication media, all power sources, railroads, airports, farms and ranches. It can force all civilians to work under government supervision, shift any segemnt of the population from one locality to another, and regulate the amount of money an individual may withdraw from banks. The Postmaster General can be directed to operate a National Registration of all people. Nixon signed the second directive on February 10, 1972.[3] This is the regional mechanism for implementing the former order. It establishes ten federal regions, which are to be governed by Regional Councils.

For some insight into the Regional Government System, one has only to look northward. In 1960, Canada established ten "planning regions." Government and university research analyzed the needs and resources of each region. Policy recommendations were made on the basis of this professional analysis. Regional Councils

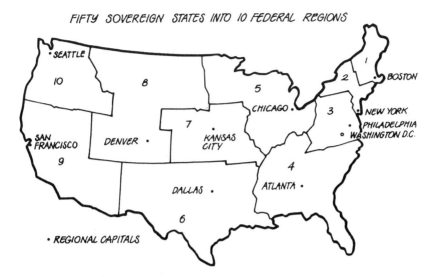

FIFTY SOVEREIGN STATES INTO 10 FEDERAL REGIONS

determined needs and resources, and advisory boards contributed the expertise to solve the problems.

Canada solved the "problems" of land-use and building development by adopting a single National Building Code, effective throughout the country. By first establishing regional control, the Constitutional issue of effecting a national code was avoided.

A similar program is now being considered for adoption of a National Building Code in the United States. An incredible number of federal agencies are working on the transfer of power to regulate building construction; a transfer from county and state levels to regional and national levels. This transfer of power can become operative through Executive Order, as explained later in this chapter, without Constitutional amendment.

OSHA is currently writing a National Building Code which will affect every citizen. For reasons explained later, the counties and states are relegating their building regulatory powers to an organization called The National Conference of States on Building Codes and Standards. (NCSBCS) This new agency is similar to another National Bureau of Standards subsidiary, The National Conference of Weights and Measures. In testimony before a Congressional subcommittee, the director of the Bureau of Standards said that the National Conference on Weights and Measures is "the model we are following in our encouragement of the National Conference of States on Building Codes and Standards,

seeking reform of the regulatory system for building construction."
Technical data used by OSHA in the formation of the new National
Code has been amassed by another committee working under the
National Bureau of Standards, the American Standards Association. FHA and HUD have also contributed to the new code
standards. Finally, the National Academy of Code Administration
is currently operating an educational and testing program to train
building officials at a number of American universities.

To answer the question, "How can Federal Regionalism be
implemented short of Executive Order?", one has only to recount
some recent legislative activity. Starting with the Intergovernmental Co-operation Act of 1968 (Public Law 90-577) which directs
a consolidation of jurisdictions, Congress has passed a series of
laws favoring regional control. Another bill (HR 11764) provided
massive funding to states which met regional "modernization"
requirements. The Land Use Policy and Planning Assistance Act
(SB 268, June 1973) requires the states to enact federal land use
policy or be denied federal grants and Revenue Sharing funds. The
bill gives the Interior Department power to restrict the use of all
areas of "critical environmental concern". The ambiguous term
"critical" may apply to any land subject to federally dictated
zoning restrictions.

Senator Carl Curtis warned us of the dangers of a national
land use law when he said, "SB 268 is an ingenious scheme to deny
the states their right to plan for land use. This elaborate and
complicated bill is drafted so that, under the guise of 'assistance,'
the federal government will take from the states one of the last
vestiges of state police power." One frightful clause in this bill
provides data-bank information on every property owner in every
state, further regulating how the property owner may use his land.
The bill paves the way for the creation of a Federal Land Czar.

Federal land control also operates under the guise of environmental protection. The recently defeated Federal Land Use Planning Bill (Jackson-Udall, June 1974) would have regulated land
division, change of land use, and building construction. Seemingly
innocuous water quality control legislation is also promoted in the
name of environmental concern. But, as a result of Water Resources Control, it is illegal for a property owner in California to
repair a leaky water pump valve. Any work performed on an

individual water system (well or pump) must be done by a licensed technician at the owner's expense.

City, county, and state governments, many of them on the verge of bankruptcy, are attracted to the promise of a federal hand-out. Local administration may receive federal "matching funds" by adopting regional legislation, such as the Administrative Procedures Act, the Intergovernmental Co-operation Act, the Model Cities Act, and Urban Renewal.

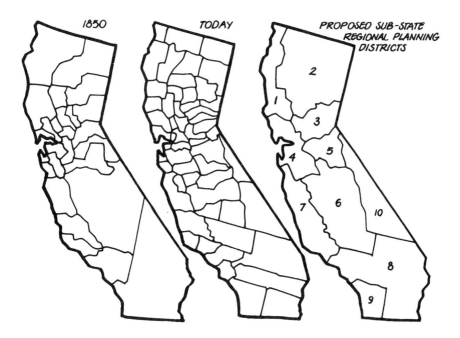

CALIFORNIA COUNTIES

Lack of space prevents us from detailing the manner in which government agencies, under the aegis of "comprehensive planning," encourage regional control. The acceptance of "comprehensive planning" qualifies local governments for federal monies, extends their tax base and provides them with greater control. Individual property rights are diminished through the resulting confiscatory taxation and land use control. Shortly, owner-builders may be denied the liberty of repairing and maintaining homeplaces, much as they are now denied the right to construct them.

Since no residential building permits are being issued in this neighborhood recently zoned for "light industrial development," the owners of this addition were forced to build surreptitiously. They first poured a slab which they called a "patio;" they then built the roof, calling it "sort of a porch;" and finally, almost overnight, they filled in the walls.

Machinations of the federal government are frightful, but there is some question as to whether regional government would be possible without a little help from private organizations. Private syndicates, responsible for the original concept of regionalism, efficiently lobby for regionalist legislation. It is one more horror story; a fitting finale to the concern for individual freedom.

Funded by a grant from the Laura Spelman Fund and an administrative management appointment from Franklin Roosevelt, a group of three far-sighted regionalists formed the Public Administrative Clearing House (PACH) in the early 1930s. The initial function of PACH included a consultation service for state and local governments with advice from experts on regional planning. By the late 1930s, PACH had expanded, incorporating other groups. Financial support came from many tax-exempt foundations, including Carnegie and Ford. The Spelman Fund put up more than a million dollars to construct a new headquarters on the University of Chicago campus at 1313 E. 60th Street. By 1953, a

Public Administration Clearing House, 1313 E. 60th St, Chicago

politically powerful conglomerate of twenty-two agencies had been established at the "1313" headquarters.

1. American Public Works Association
2. Municipal Finance Officers Association
3. Public Personnel Association
4. National Association of Attorneys General
5. National Governor's Conference
6. International City Managers' Association
7. American Municipal Association
8. American Committee for International Municipal Co-operation
9. Council of State Governments
10. National Association of Housing and Redevelopment Officials
11. Public Administration Service
12. National Association of Assessing Officers
13. American Society of Planning Officials
14. Federation of Tax Administrators
15. American Society for Public Administration
16. National Association of State Budget Officers
17. National Association of State Purchasing Officials
18. National Institute of Municipal Clerks
19. National Legislative Conference

20. Conference of Chief Justices
21. Interstate Clearing House on Mental Health
22. American Public Welfare Association

In recent years, four more influential organizations were added to the 1313 roster: The National Association of Counties (NACO), the National League of Cities (NLC), the U.S. Conference of Mayors (USCM), and—yes—the Building Officials Conference of America (BOCA). One of the first orders of business for this conglomerate was the promotion of the infamous Intergovernmental Co-operation Act. In 1971, the Council of State Governments prepared a survey which showed that only a dozen states had not adopted this act. (See Appendix C)

Not all states and counties have enjoyed a happy marriage under the act. The Tahoe Regional Planning Agency instituted by California and Nevada in 1969, became the first regional planning body to operate in California. Congress approved the merger, forming a five-county bi-state region. El Dorado County came to resent the merger and the subsequent usurpation of local sovereignty. The county dropped its membership in the National Association of Counties, claiming in the words of Supervisor Johnson, "Your alteration of our local elected county government and your promotion of appointed regional government, not autorized by the voters, are not at all acceptable to our Board. We have intimate experience with the tyranny of appointed regional government, as one such encompasses part of our county at Lake Tahoe. This move to centralize government, subordinating elected local government, is not to our liking."

The El Dorado Board of Supervisors filed a resolution calling for an investigation of the Federal Regionalism concept. We are reproducing this resolution (See Appendix D) in the hope that it might serve as a precept for other counties in their struggle to regain homerule.

Experiences teaches that none can guide the community;

The community is a collaboration of forces; such as,
thought shows, it cannot be led by the strength of one man.

To order it is to set it in disorder;

To fix it is to unsettle it.

For the conduct of the individual changes:
Here goes forward, there draws back;
Here shows warmth, there reveals cold;
Here exerts strength, there displays weakness;
Here stirs passion, there brings peace.

And so:
The perfected one shuns desire for power,
shuns the lure of power,
shuns the glamour of power.

Lao Tze, 6th century B. C.

Conclusion

All the words and illustrations in this book may be condensed into one concluding premise: everyone should be free to build a home as long as, in the process, the rights of others are protected. It may be necessary and desirable to regulate commercial building, but regulation should not automatically include and arbitrarily inhibit individual home builders. If, at the moment they begin home construction projects, owner-builders do not know best how to create those structures, we feel they will profit in the learning derived from the experience. Allowed freedom of choice in a climate relieved of miseducation and useless restriction, the human community can and will make building decisions meaningful for itself.

The power to make choices in behalf of oneself and one's community has passed from the condition of decentralized personal autonomy where "people know best" to that state in which control is centralized in a specialized bureaucracy presuming to know what is best for all people.

Housing is merely one social industry that has been successfully usurped by commercial interests and government control. Other social institutions, similarly coerced, include education, agriculture and health. State-controlled "educational" facilities are in the business of teaching the production and consumption of goods and services, instead of instructing people in personal skills applicable to self-reliance. In agriculture, emphasis is placed on capital-based machine-intensive methods instead of on people-based labor-intensive methods. And finally, the medical profession has become the great expropriator of human health. No other profession has been so successful in the monopolization of its particular specialty.

Building professionals, teachers, agribusinessmen and doctors have all contributed their part in reducing modern man to a sub-human condition of dependence and ineptitude. Our thesis merely suggests that, insofar as human shelter is concerned, what is needed is a restoration of confidence in the concept of individual libery and initiative employed in the creation of a fitting dwelling place. The relaxation of building regulations for owner-builders will go far toward reviving this inalienable right to self-determination. To this end, we have attempted to question and to re-think the role of the bureaucratic structure which enforces building restriction.

If the alternative code requirements which we propose for owner-building appear incomplete or impractical in some respects, we can only argue that this has been a ground-breaking endeavor on our part. As yet, there exists no large-scale code-reform movement upon which to draw, and certainly there exists no inter-disciplinary attempt by the building industry or by government to reform the code. We are hopeful that the first printing of this book will foster direct contact between the authors and the 5,000 readers of this edition. All reader feedback will be evaluated, responded to and, with permission, incorporated into future editions.

United Stand of Mendocino has expressed a willingness to serve as a clearinghouse for communication on code reform, alternative sewage systems, and related land-use issues. Readers of this book are encouraged to communicate on these subjects with United Stand, P.O. Box 191, Potter Valley, CA 95469. United Stand is public-supported so donations will be welcome. We hope such a clearinghouse will promote an owner-builder awareness which will help to return the choice of shelter to the individual. We have witnessed the effect that a small organization can have on code reform in one section of this country. It is now opportune to expand our concern to include owner-builders everywhere.

It is our hope that a constitutional challenge to uniform building codes can be accomplished through increased public knowledge of these laws. A decision must be extracted which clearly elucidates the limits of government to control the construction of a home for oneself. Monte Marshall's attempt in Eugene, Oregon, failed for lack of finances and public support, and United Stand's constitutional questions were ignored by the justice court. (Legal briefs of both cases are available through United Stand). The possibility still exists, however, that a case could be carried to the federal judiciary. An owner-builder "conspiracy" could make it happen.

Communication with the authors can be made through P.O. Box 550, Oakhurst, CA 93644.

Appendix A

DEMOLITION AGREEMENT

This agreement executed by and between the Property Owner, below named and the Wrecker-Salvager, below named, provides as follows:

RECITALS

1. Property Owner:_____

2. Wrecker-Salvager:_____

3. Location of Property:_____

_____

4. Description of Structure:_____

_____

5. Consideration: Amount:_____, paid by_____

to:_____

6. Length of Time to be completed:_____

NOW THEREFORE IT IS MUTUALLY AGREED AS FOLLOWS:

1. That Property Owner shall permit the demolition of the structure described above on the property described above and Wrecker-Salvager agrees to demolish the same in the length of time set forth above.

2. Wrecker-Salvager agrees to clean up the site of the building and agrees to remove all rubbish and debris except the removal of any foundations, and except as otherwise permitted herein: Exceptions:_____

_____

3. Wrecker-Salvager shall have the right to salvage all materials taken from the building except as follows: Exceptions_____

_____

4. The consideration in the amount set forth above in Paragraph 5 of the Recitals in the amount set forth in Paragraph 5 is to be paid by the person so stipulated to the person so named in Paragraph 5.

WAIVER OF LIABILITY AND HOLD HARMLESS

5. Wrecker-Salvager hereby agrees to waive any and all liability against the Property Owner for any actual or potential liability arising from accidents which occur during the demolition of the building.

6. Wrecker-Salvager further agrees that he shall hold the Property Owner harmless from any liability accrued as a result of injury to workman provided by the Wrecker Salvager, or in the employee of the Wrecker-Salvager, or acting as his individual contractors.

7. All reference to Property Owner, Wrecker-Salvager, Contractor and length of time for completion of this contract hereto are incorporated by reference as the respective directions set forth in the Recitals set forth herein above.

8. PROPERTY OWNERS   WRECKER-SALVAGERS

   DATE:_____   DATE:_____

   _____   _____

   _____   _____

   _____   _____

Appendix B

The following is a complete cost breakdown of the house pictured on page 86 of the text. The house was built to code on a limited budget during the period 1971 - 1973. Standard construction methods and standard materials were used throughout. All materials were purchased new unless otherwise noted. The builder was extremely concerned with keeping the cost of the house as low as possible so every opportunity was taken to find and use the most inexpensive materials.

Building permit for 926 sq.ft. house . . . . . . $ 63.00

Foundation . . . . $ 261.69

4 yds. readymix concrete (5 sack)	$ 81.20
327 6"x8"x16" concrete blocks	98.30
block cartage	15.60
form lumber(a burn)	19.60
materials for mortar	36.30
anchor bolts	9.69
	$261.69

Framing lumber $1,145.49

1700 board feet utility 2"x8" tongue and groove fir for subfloor	$158.01
3040 board feet standard and better fir - 2"x4", 2"x6", 4"x4", 4"x6", and 4"x8"	582.48
3000 board feet 2"x6" tongue and groove #200 hemlock for ceilings	405.00
	$1145.49

Exterior walls . . . . $ 376.26

40 sheets 4'x8'x3/8" CDX plywood	$103.65
13 squares #1 cedar shingles	272.61
	$376.26

Windows . . . . $ 151.49

3 used wooden sash for bathroom	$ 10.50
15 used wooden casement sash with hardware	38.00
3 used industrial steel sash	12.00
replacement glass, putty, clips, etc.	29.95
finish lumber for frames	61.04
	$151.49

```
Doors . . . . . . . . . . . . . . . . . . . . . . . .  $   58.32
      2 used exterior doors with hardware   $ 24.50
      2 used interior doors with hardware     10.00
      finish lumber for frames                23.82
                                            $ 58.32

Roof . . . . . . . . . . . . . . . . . . . . . . . .  $  267.59
      6 squares 1" rigid insulation         $ 75.96
      7 squares composition shingles          80.15
      3½ squares #1 cedar shingles            70.00
      gutters, flashing, roof jacks, etc.     42.48
                                            $267.59

Heating system . . . . . . . . . . . . . . . . . .  $  164.93
      used wood heat stove                  $ 80.00
      8"x33" metalbestos flue kit with roof
        jack and storm collar                 45.59
      custom-made 8"x6' galvanized chimney
        with tie-downs: custom-made
        interior cover plate: 6" to 8"
      increaser                               39.34
                                            $ 84.93

Electrical . . . . . . . . . . . . . . . . . . . . .  $  242.12
      wire: 750' 12/2wg ($50.43), 45' 6/3wg
        ($22.05), misc. ($9.55)             $ 82.03
      47 receptacles, switches, and light
        sockets                               45.83
      200 amp service entrance with wire,
        breakers, meter base, weatherhead     85.37
      miscellaneous rods, clamps, covers,
        nuts, etc.                            18.89
      permits                                 10.00
                                            $242.12

Plumbing . . . . . . . . . . . . . . . . . . . . . .  $  424.07
      materials for ABS plastic drain,
        waste, vent system rough-in         $ 96.18
      materials for copper supply system
        rough-in                              67.10
      55 gal. electric hot water heater
        and plumbing fittings                 67.90
      flush toilet and fittings               37.48
      double stainless steel kitchen sink
        and fittings                          50.14
      5' porcelain tub and fittings           68.36
      shower fittings                          8.04
      crockery lavatory (used) and fittings   21.67
      outdoor faucets                          7.50
                                            $424.07

Finish floor . . . . . . . . . . . . . . . . . . . .  $  203.40
      2200 board feet #3 (reject) 1"x4"
        tongue and groove fir flooring      $150.00
      rental of nailing machine (1 week)       7.00
      special non-split, toothed nails        25.90
      rental of floor sanders with paper      20.50
                                            $203.40
```

```
Interior walls . . . . . . . . . . . . . . . . .  $   302.97
    9 rolls (630 sq. ft.) 3½" foil-
       backed wall insulation          $ 48.09
    29 sheets ½"x4'x8' sheetrock for
       living, dining and bedrooms        52.11
    labor for taping sheetrock          105.56
    310 board feet 1"x4" roughsawn cedar
       for halls and stairway walls       50.00
    210 board feet B & better beveled
       cedar siding in 3' lengths for
       kitchen                           15.75
    233 board feet 1"x10" utility &
       better roughsawn cedar for bath    31.46
                                        $302.97

Finish lumber . . . . . . . . . . . . . . . . .  $   206.06
    materials for cabinets            $ 83.00
    clear fir treads and risers for
       eight 36" wide stairs             35.16
    clear vertical grain fir for trim    83.60
                                       $206.06

Miscellaneous . . . . . . . . . . . . . . . . .  $   272.87
    nails                             $ 37.78
    15 pound felt                       33.07
    caulk                               13.33
    paint                               83.18
    saw blade sharpening                19.95
    other                               85.56
                                       $272.87

COST of HOUSE, exclusive of its
    attachments and supporting systems which
    are itemized in the following list . . . . . . $4,140.26


Water supply system . . . . . . . . . . . . . .  $   418.73
    one horse shallow well pump with
       jet and 40 gal. pressure tank   $184.86
    450 gallon cylindrical storage tank
       home-made with cedar 2"x4"x6'
       boards bound with steel hoops     88.04
    pump house and pump mount with slab
       floor, cedar walls, shingle roof  28.80
    fittings and valves                  28.24
    200 feet 1¼" 125 lb. plastic pipe    46.72
    200 feet 10/2wg underground wire,
       20 amp breaker, electrical boxes  42.07
                                       $418.73

Septic system . . . . . . . . . . . . . . . . .  $   375.00
    contracted system with 140' field,
       30' tight line, 1000 gal. tank  $370.00
    septic permit                         5.00
                                       $375.00
```

```
Outside deck . . . . . . . . . . . . . . . . . . .$   142.99
        900 board feet used 2"x12" and
            4"x8" fir                        $ 83.00
        17 12"x12" pier blocks                 16.50
        bolts, nuts, washers                   33.49
        50 lbs. 8" grooved deck spikes         10.00
                                             $142.99

Driveway . . . . . . . . . . . . . . . . . . . . .$    61.50
        26 tons 3" no minus crushed rock    $ 36.50
        10 tons 1½" minus crushed rock
            delivered                          35.00
                                            $ 61.50


SUBTOTAL of supporting systems . . . . . . . . .  $   998.22


GRAND TOTAL . . . . . . . . . . . . . . . . . . .$5,138.48
```

Appendix C

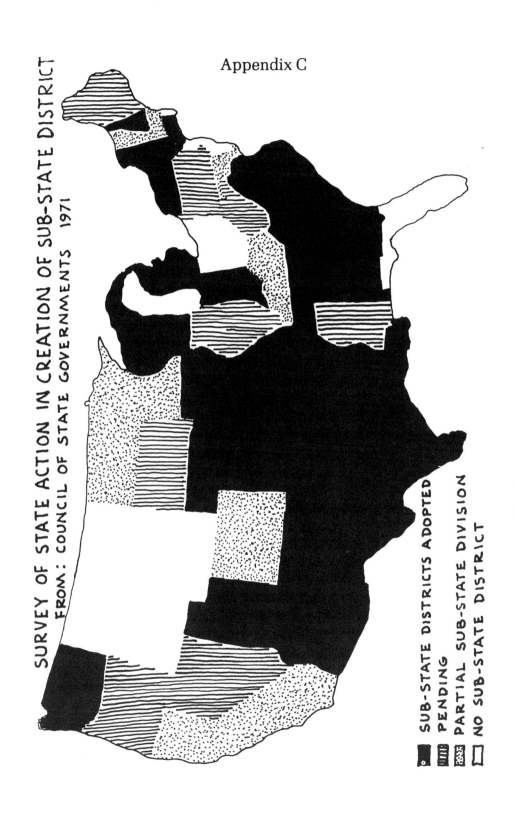

SURVEY OF STATE ACTION IN CREATION OF SUB-STATE DISTRICT
FROM: COUNCIL OF STATE GOVERNMENTS 1971

SUB-STATE DISTRICTS ADOPTED
PENDING
PARTIAL SUB-STATE DIVISION
NO SUB-STATE DISTRICT

Appendix D

NS:mal.
10-16-73

RESOLUTION No. 487-73

OF THE BOARD OF SUPERVISORS OF THE COUNTY OF EL DORADO

WHEREAS, the El Dorado County Board of Supervisors is on record affirming support of the principle of local representative government, elected by popular vote of the citizens governed; and

WHEREAS, El Dorado County, through the use of existing methods and structures of government, has demonstrated that cooperation with neighboring counties and cities can solve mutual problems; and

WHEREAS, there is increasing evidence of a determined effort toward regional redistricting as a substitute for such cooperation, which effort does not originate at the local level, and appears to be developing into a direct attack on the autonomy of city and county government; and

WHEREAS, under the direction of the California Council on Inter-governmental Relations (an appointed body), the State has been divided into arbitrary multi-county regions, (substate regionals), presumably with appointed regional councils replacing authority previously and properly reserved to elected municipal and county officials; and

WHEREAS, these substate regionals are intended to become local agencies for the administration of state and federal programs, and will not represent the citizens in the local areas; and

WHEREAS, this movement is not confined to the State of California, but is taking place in other states as well, and all such substate regionals interlock with the division of the United States into Ten Standard Federal Regions, as mandated by the President in an Executive Order (EO #11647, 12 February 1972) which placed California with Nevada and Arizona in "Region Nine" without the knowledge or consent of the citizens; and

WHEREAS, it would appear that EO #11647 is in direct violation of Article IV, Sections 3 and 4 of the Constitution of the United States and of the Tenth Amendment, as well as Article 1, Sections 2, 22, 23, and Article 3, Section 1 of the California Constitution

WHERES, the evident goal of the regionalization of local, state and federal governments is centralization of power and authority, which rightfully and constitutionally belongs to these several governments; transference of custody of the public purse to appointed officials; and, usurpation of the rights and freedoms of the citizens which are guaranteed by the Constitution of the United States and the Constitutions of the several states, including the State of California,

NOW, THEREFORE, BE IT RESOLVED by the Board of Supervisors of the County of El Dorado in the State of California, that the evidence in support of the above recitals is sufficiently strong to warrant immediate action; that fulfillment of their solemn oath of office to support and defend the Constitutions of the United States and of the State of California requires that this Board make known to all whom it may concern that, in the course of conducting the business of El Dorado County, matters have come to their attention which indicates the substance of the above to be true, and

1) that copies of this resolution be sent to the Boards of Supervisors of each and all of the several counties in the State of California, to the Sheriff of each county and to the County Supervisors Association of California.

2) that the Boards of Supervisors of the other counties be, and they are hereby requested to join with the El Dorado County Board in demanding of all persons responsible that no further action of any nature whatsoever be taken on any phase of this substate redistricting until such time as there can be a determination made of the desires and will of the several counties and their citizens with regard to its continuance.

3) that the El Dorado County Board of Supervisors invites suggestions from other counties as to methods of determining necessary procedures directed toward holding a joint investigation into this entire matter to provide opportunity for all persons having information and/or evidence of misrepresentation, fraud, conspiracy or sedition, or any other illegal activity connected with this movement of regionalization, to be heard.

4) that the El Dorado County Board urges other counties to use every means available to them to manifest the urgency of this matter and to inform their citizens of this concern; such means should include consideration of adoption of a resolution similar to this as evidence to those who represent their citizens at the state and federal levels of determination to insure that the solution to the problems which are the stated basis for this proposal is not a greater ill than the problem.

5) that copies of this resolution also be sent to State Senator Clare Berryhill, Assemblyman Eugene Chappie, the Hon. Ralph C. Dills, Chairman of the State Senate Governmental Organization Committee, the Hon. Newton R. Russell, Chairman of the State Assembly Government Administration Committee, the Hon. Leon D. Ralph, Chairman of the Assembly Governmental Organization Committee, Senator Milton Marks and Assemblyman John T. Knox, Chairman of the respective Local Government Committees, United States Senators Alan Cranston and John Tunney, Congressman Harold T. Johnson and the Governor and Lieutenant Governor of the State of California.

PASSED AND ADOPTED by the Board of Supervisors of the County of El Dorado at a regular meeting of said Board, held on the ...16th...... day of ....October............., 19..73..., by the following vote of said Board:

ATTEST:

CARL A. KELLY, County Clerk and ex-officio
Clerk of the Board of Supervisors

By ....
　　　　　　Deputy Clerk

Ayes: Franklin K. Lane, William V.D. Johnson, W.P. Walker, Raymond E. Lawyer

Noes: None

Absent: Thomas L. Stewart

....
Chairman, Board of Supervisors　　(end)

Footnotes

SECTION ONE: THE CODE

1. Mood, Eric. "The Development, Objective, and Adequacy of Current Housing Code Standards." Housing Code Standards, Three Critical Studies, a report prepared for the National Commission on Urban Problems. Washington, D.C.: 1969, pp. 45-49.

Chapter 1: An Overview

1. Bureau of the Census, Department of Commerce, with the Department of Housing and Urban Development. Construction Reports C-25 Series. Washington, D.C.: U.S. Govt. Printing Office, 1963-69.

2. Allen, Edward, ed. The Responsive House. Cambridge: MIT Press, 1974, pp. 46-47.

3. Jung, Carl. Memories, Dreams, Reflections. New York: Viking Press, 1957, p. 225.

4. Kaufman, Reinhard. Schrift der Galerie Renate Bourkes. A manifesto read in the Abbey of Seckau, Wiesbaden, July 4, 1958.

Chapter 2: History

1. Colling, R.C. and Cal Colling, eds. Modern Building Inspection. Los Angeles: Building Standards Monthly Publishing Co., 1950, p. 12.

2. Sanderson, Richard L. Codes and Code Administration. Chicago: Building Officials Conference of America, Inc. 1969, pp. 38-39.

3. Thompson, George N. Preparation and Revision of Building Codes. U.S. Department of Commerce, National Bureau of Standards, Building Materials and Structures Report BNS 116. Washington, D.C.: U.S. Govt. Printing Office, 1949, p. 2.

4. National Commission on Urban Problems. Building the American City, Report of the National Commission of Urban Problems to the Congress and to the President of the United States. Washington, D.C.: U.S. Govt. Printing Office, 1968, p. 266.

5. Sanderson, op. cit., p. 14

Chapter 3 ; Extent

1. Sanderson, op. cit., 9. 43

2. National Commission on Urban Problems, op. cit., p. 257.

3. Ibid., p. 259.

4. Wood, Edith Elmer. Recent Trends in American Housing. New York: Macmillan, 1931, p. 123.

Chapter 4: Failures

1. San Francisco Chronicle, March 1974, quoting Department of Commerce statistics.

2. Rivkin, Steven R. Courting Change: Using Litigation to Reform Local Building Codes." Rutgers Law Review, vol. 26 [1973], p. 774.

Chapter 5: Safe and Sanitary

1. Love, Sam. An Idea in Need of Rethinking: the Flush Toilet." Smithsonian Magazine [April, 1975), p. 62.

2. Wagner and Lanoix. Excrete Disposal for Rural Areas and Small Communities. Geneva: World Health Organization, 1958.

SECTION TWO: THE OWNER-BUILDER

Chapter 6: A Profile

1. Rapoport, Amos. House Form and Culture. Englewood Cliffs, N.J.: Prentice-Hall, 1969, pp. 18-45.

2. The elements of the "Barn style" are: a large central space with high ceilings and usually including kitchen, dining, and living areas; a second floor with bedrooms or sleeping lofts; and an abundance of exposed wood.

Chapter 8: Construction

1. Woodward, G.E. Woodward's Country Homes. New York; 1869, p. 156.

SECTION THREE: THE OWNER-BUILDER AND THE CODE

Chapter 10: The Western Scene

1. Van der Zee. Canyon. New York: Harcourt Brace Johanovich, 1971, p. 31.

2. Ibid., p. 161.

3. Thoele, Mike. "The Artist vs. the Code." Eugene Register-Guard, April 6, 1975.

Chapter 11: United Stand

1. Real, James, "California Hillbillies Fight Back! New Times Magazine [November 29, 1974], p. 38.

2. Ibid., p. 36.

Chapter 13: Evasion

1. Oliver, Paul, ed. Shelter and Society. New York: Praeger, 1969, p. 137.

Chapter 14: The Future

1. Hindman, Jo. The Metrocats. Caldwell, Idaho: Coxton Printers, 1974, p. 62.

2. Federal Register. October 30, 1969.

3. Ibid., February 10, 1972.